The

Final
Mission

Decorations Awarded to Lt. Col. Henry Supchak

Distinguished Flying Cross

Air Medal (six times)

Purple Heart

Prisoner of War Medal

World War II Victory Medal

*European-African-Middle Eastern Campaign
Medal (with Service Stars)*

American Campaign Medal

The Final Mission

A Boy, a Pilot, and a World at War

Elizabeth Hoban *and*
Lt. Col. Henry Supchak

WESTHOLME
Yardley

Westholme Publishing, LLC
904 Edgewood Road
Yardley, Pennsylvania 19067
Visit our Web site at www.westholmepublishing.com

First Printing May 2012
10 9 8 7 6 5 4 3 2 1

ISBN: 978-1-59416-155-1

Also available as an eBook.

Printed in the United States of America.

In loving memory of
Gene Elizabeth Supchak

War is that mad game the world so loves to play.

—Jonathan Swift

CONTENTS

Author's Note

This book is based on interviews with my father and the more than one thousand handwritten pages composed by him over the past thirty years in his attempt to understand his posttraumatic stress disorder. Once we learned of the Austrian man who recalled my father during World War II and independently sought to find him, I was able to interview him in that country with the assistance of Jakob Mayer so that his history could be placed in the context of the events in my father's life. Statistical information comes from official American records, while additional information about the German Stalag Luft III and Stalag VIIA prison camps comes from *The Longest Mission*, a privately printed commemorative book published by The Association of Former Prisoners of Stalag Luft III.

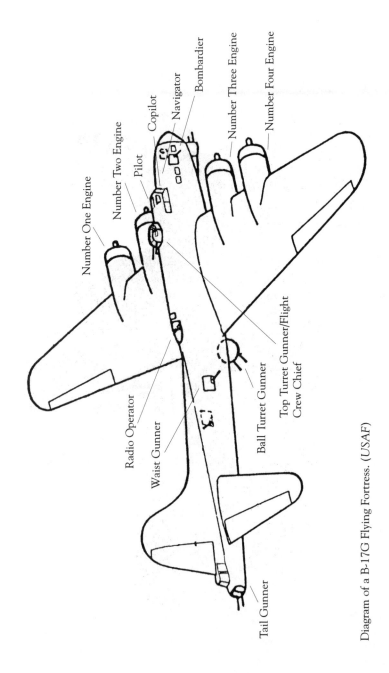

Number One Engine

Number Two Engine

Pilot

Copilot

Navigator

Bombardier

Number Three Engine

Number Four Engine

Radio Operator

Waist Gunner

Ball Turret Gunner

Top Turret Gunner/Flight
Crew Chief

Tail Gunner

Diagram of a B-17G Flying Fortress. (USAF)

Priority Gal's Crew (April 1944–July 1944)

PILOT: Lt. Henry Supchak

COPILOT: Lt. John Karlac

NAVIGATOR: Lt. Robert "Kruz" Krusan/
Lt. Stewart Feinman

BOMBARDIER: Lt. Wilson Leahy

FLIGHT CREW CHIEF AND
TOP TURRET GUNNER: Tech/Sgt. Glenn Thomas

RADIO OPERATOR–GUNNER: Sgt. Michael Hettler/
Sgt. Kenneth Taylor

TAIL GUNNER: Sgt. William Sheppard

WAIST GUNNER: Sgt. Anthony Skorpik

BALL TURRET GUNNER: Sgt. Guy "Rocco" La Rocco

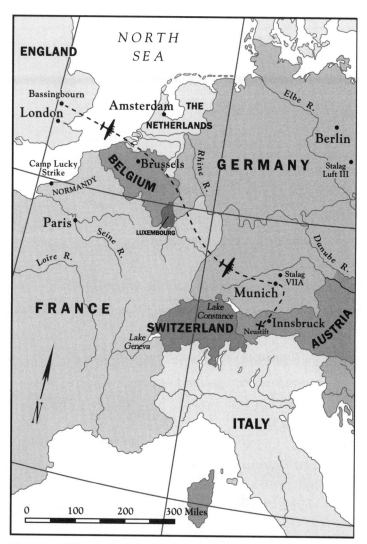

The route of *Priority Gal*'s final flight.

PROLOGUE

6,000 feet over Neustift, Austria
July 31, 1944, 1130 hours

I was on my own in a fatal situation. A few moments earlier, with both starboard engines of my B-17 on fire, I ordered my crew of eight men to bail out. For the first time in thirty-three air-combat missions, I was alone in a crippled bomber with no hope of reaching England or the neutrality of the Swiss border.

Dark, acrid smoke seeped into the cockpit, causing my eyes to burn. I took a swallow of water from my thermos, but it didn't quench my thickening thirst. A painful throb and a widening bloodstain surrounded the chunk of shrapnel embedded in my right knee. When the plane's altitude dropped below six thousand feet, I knew I had about ninety seconds to escape.

I released myself from the seat and glanced up through the caustic fumes enveloping the cockpit.

Priority Gal was headed straight toward a village at the base of the Alps. Her current course would wipe out most of the town and its residents. Although several Nazi soldiers would also be eliminated in the process, I wasn't about to kill innocent civilians.

Instinctively, I jumped back in the seat and readjusted the controls to a maximum leftward flight path and flipped the wing trim tabs. Forcing the extreme turn was not an easy task, and it took some muscle and no room to spare to get my *Gal* to make a ninety-degree turn. Her riveted metal seams groaned in protest to the drastic maneuver, but she cooperated and veered clear of the village. Common to the sheer terrain of the Alps, *Priority Gal* caught an updraft on the back end of the turn. She gained some altitude, but would it give the bomber enough weightlessness for me to bail out before she crashed into the mountains dead ahead?

I lowered myself from the cockpit and into the nose section while I readied my harness pack for bailout. Chute on and nearing the hatch, I said a quick goodbye to my Army Colt .45 and tossed it out the opening. I knew better than to give the Nazis a reason to execute me on the spot. Before I could exit the bomber, *Priority Gal* went into a spin and gravitational force threw me back, pinning me to the floor. My heart tried boxing its way out of my chest while I struggled to free myself from the invisible menace. All the while an acute burning sensation was spreading through my injured leg. I pushed away images of my loved ones and faced the life or death moment at hand.

Using every ounce of strength I could muster, I grappled my way toward the hatch. When I finally grabbed the opening, blood stained the fingertips of my gloves. My body seemed to give out less than an arm's length from the hatch. *Priority Gal* had been my loyal compatriot. She had always defied gravity, and she would never allow it to defeat me.

As if by a miracle, the centrifugal force abated for a split second, and I dropped through the square opening in a dizzying free fall. Air currents burst through my nose and mouth, filling my lungs. I pulled the rip cord of my chute, felt a punch to the chin and a kick to the crotch when the canopy billowed, and I began my slow descent.

Within seconds, my beloved *Priority Gal* crashed into a mountainside ravine and exploded—her final resting place and almost my own. What awaited me when I landed in the freshly thatched pasture below was uncertain. In that brief shard of time, after saying a solemn goodbye to my *Gal*, I drifted on warm breezes, simply grateful to be alive.

Lt. Henry Supchak at the controls of *Priority Gal* in 1944. (*Author*)

PART ONE

The Pilot

ONE

Bassingbourn, England
July 31, 1944, 0500 hours

DAYLIGHT MADE AN EARLY DEBUT, SUGGESTING clear flying conditions, but I knew the weather could change before I downed my second cup of coffee. After several months in England, I got used to stretches of time when the sun was something of an enigma. The mess hall was crowded with flight crews and typically quiet at five in the morning when I placed my breakfast order.

"Morning, Sergeant Lang. Three eggs over medium, toast well done, coffee straight up." I saluted the chef and swallowed down an orange juice before the glass even hit my tray. Then I reached for a second while I stood in the mess line and waited for my chow.

"Three eggs this morning, really, sir?" Sergeant Lang was a good guy and an excellent chef with a

Texas twang in his voice. "You not eat yesterday, or wha—?"

"I'm a growing boy, Chief." I tried to recall the previous day's menu when a deep voice came up behind me, tray in hand, and cutting in line as usual.

"Missed you at the club last night, Lieutenant."

I rolled my eyes, turned and smiled in spite of myself. "You're up early this morning, Kruz, what gives?" I turned back and took the plate from the cook's outstretched hand and nodded a thank you.

Sergeant Lang offered up a "good luck" by way of salute, and I smiled. There were so many men and women who served the Allied forces by keeping the troops supplied, fed, and ready, and deserved to be recognized for their vital roles. This cowboy was one of them.

"Remind me never to offer to buy you breakfast when we get back to the states," Krusan chuckled when he saw my full plate. He turned to the chef. "Black coffee and a buttered English muffin, pal."

"So now I'm your pal. Wasn't it just last night you sold me down the river for a pair of threes?" While the two of them feigned bickering, Krusan waited for his muffin, and I made my way to a seat.

Lieutenant Bob Krusan, "Kruz" for short, had the well-deserved reputation for being one of the sharpest navigators in the European theater. We'd been friends back in the states from the time we were assigned together and had flown more than thirty missions in and out of Germany. I trusted and loved the man. As a pilot, I figured who better to get along with than my navigator?

"Damnedest thing, me having one more mission than you," Krusan lamented while he stirred sugar in his coffee. "They credited me for that training detachment I did when we first got here, but I have to say, I'm relieved to be sitting this one out. I nearly lost my shirt last night in that poker game and was relegated to rotgut whiskey. Got a headache the size of Montana." He was great at the airman bravado, but I knew better. He didn't have to get up at all that day. Krusan came to breakfast to wish me luck, as I would have done for him had the situation been reversed.

He took a swig of coffee and winced, a common reaction from the bitter burn of the government-issued beverage, then glanced down at my nearly empty plate. Not one to mince words, he blew out a long whistle. "Jeez, Lieutenant, you have a tape worm?"

"Just hungry, I guess." I changed the subject to the previous day. "Colonel Terry told me yesterday after our Ops meeting he was planning a final mission for us this Thursday so we can finish together. He says there's a transport flight leaving Heathrow at 0400 hours on Sunday, destination New York, and he wants us both on that flight. Says he can't wait to get rid of us, we've been nothing but a pain in the butt." I chuckled at the memory of my conversation with the commanding officer of the 91st Bomb Group,

Colonel Henry W. Terry, a man I respected immensely. He always kept his eye on the prize, getting his crews back from their missions in one piece. "I can tell you this much: I'm ready to return to my old life, whatever's left of it anyway, no offense to England."

I wasn't sure what awaited me when I got back home, home being Nanticoke, Pennsylvania. None of us really knew how we would be welcomed home, but we all fantasized about our personal ticker-tape parade, the key to the city, and an endless stream of pride. As my time to return stateside drew closer, I realized pomp and circumstance was for winning baseball teams and movie stars, and it would be business as usual within a couple of days back home. That was fine by me; the humdrum mediocrity of my mom's Sunday dinners and changing the oil in my dad's Ford was just the tedium I needed at that point. I missed the commonality of my own family and friends.

I had to admit, the English treated the American servicemen like family, always bending over backward to show appreciation for our participation in the war effort. Even amid a world war, hospitality and virtue never escaped them. We had given the British ample reason to despise us; we drank their booze, stole their women, and were, generally speaking, an obnoxious bunch. They tolerated our presence, but were also anxious to get back to life as they knew it before American servicemen invaded their country.

I knew no matter what lay ahead for me back in the states, I was proud I had served my country, my world, in this case. Someday, maybe I'd revisit England after this dreadful war was over. For now, I couldn't wait to say adios to Europe.

"Listen, sir, with all due respect." Krusan paused, caught my eye, and winked at me. "None of us knows what will happen tomorrow. Uncle Sam could tack on an extra ten missions again." He blew out an exasperated sigh. "The British are so uptight about this war—it's as if it's their war; they wear it on their sleeves and I get that, but what gets my goat is they're so much smarter than we are. You don't hear British radio programs discussing Allied strategies. Here we got the *Memphis Belle* flying all over the United States like an advertisement bragging about her twenty-five missions, giving people tours. Meanwhile, we're over here doing more missions before we can go home because those fools are giving away all our secrets. How many Nazis do you think have taken tours and photos inside *Memphis Belle*? Huh?" He didn't wait for my answer. "If you ask me, the wrong guys are getting all the glory. I'd say it's almost laughable if I didn't have one more dance with His Majesty's reaper."

"Get over yourself, Kruz. If you love the U.S. of A., you take the good with the bad. Besides, it's in the officer's training manual—Uncle Sam owns you." I winked back at my friend sitting across from me; he could've been my brother. "Until you and I are sharing a drink in some stateside dive, we are property of the government."

"Well, the way I see it, Lieutenant, that drink is right around the corner for the two of us, eye on the prize, eye on the prize." Krusan yawned and stretched his arms.

I swallowed the last bit of lukewarm coffee, wiped my mouth with the white paper napkin, and dropped it to the plate where it tented, as if in surrender to the conversation. Standing, I affectionately squeezed Krusan's shoulder, then picked up my tray and headed for the door, anticipating a parting shot from my navigator.

"Good luck with Lieutenant Feinman. Obviously he's nowhere near the caliber of navigator I am, nor does he possess my dynamic charm, but he'll do. Checked him out—top of his squadron back home."

I appreciated the sanctioning of his replacement for the mission, but of course I had checked the novice navigator out myself. I wasn't taking any chances on my swan-song flights, not on anyone's life.

"Enjoy your briefing, sir, and think of me lounging in the officer's club, drinking my third cup of crapola coffee, the final mug with a shot of cheap whiskey, while I leisurely read whatever British rag I can dredge up. The highlight of my day will boil down to whether or not I get a hot lunch. I'm not even thirty and I'm already fifty."

I paused long enough to see Krusan get up and shuffle to the kitchen for what I assumed was more of the burnt brew. He gave a lazy salute in my direction that said: *See you on the other side*. True to form, I returned the gesture—so many inane responses, inside jokes, if you will, at that point in our military career. I left the mess hall without another glance back, and without considering the possibility that I'd never see Lieutenant Krusan again.

TWO

THE BRIEFING AREA OF THE QUONSET HUT thrummed with various nervous conversations. The day's maps and missions had yet to be revealed, still hidden behind the black curtain at the front of the briefing area. Cigarette smoke swirled upward toward the exposed ceiling bulbs, creating eerie ghostlike images, and nicotine permeated the air, so even if you didn't smoke, you did. It was like a bar, but without the booze and broads. Tensions ran high, and the laughter was low and guarded.

I took my seat second row back as was expected, according to some unwritten, ranked seating chart. Other than what I had been told about Lt. Stewart Feinman, my substitute navigator, I had never met him, so I'd have to seek him out after the briefing. The seat to my right was empty, but I knew

Lieutenant John Karlac would eventually show up with the attitude that war was an inconvenience, and he'd rather be golfing. I guess to a certain extent he was right. We were trained to believe war was a necessary evil—kill or be killed. But it didn't mean we had to like it.

Glancing around the room, I spotted my bombardier, Lt. Wilson Leahy, chatting it up with the only woman in the room. I recognized her as the commander's very married secretary. Leahy stood at ease, his right leg casually slung over the back of a metal folding chair, as if waiting for a shoe shine. I had met his wife back in the states, a gorgeous Hollywood starlet, Jodi, but we were a world away from the women in our lives. Besides, it was all just innocent banter. The women, though few and far between, were a pleasant distraction.

Leahy was a cool customer, and he knew it. If the crew needed comic relief, he never let them down. I admired him because he was dead-on when it came to homing in on the target. He was the only man on my crew I fully trusted with the gears. There came a point in every mission when he had the target in the crosshairs, and I had to temporarily transfer the controls to him. It wasn't long, maybe minutes, but my chest always ached afterward, as if I held my breath the whole time. I had to trust the guy.

Moreover, I lauded the man for the job he did on every mission. Lieutenant Leahy had the daunting responsibility of temporarily flying the plane while bombing the target. Then, afterward, he'd run the catwalk to check the bomb bay and make certain no bombs had remained behind. There were times Leahy had to climb down into the bomb bay because the doors were jammed, and if the lower hatch was open, we couldn't land. Having a malfunctioning armed bomb ten thousand feet up was never a good situation, either. On several occasions, he hung over the catwalk and disarmed a defective bomb. Womanizer or not, Leahy was loyal to *Priority Gal* and never complained when he did his dicey job.

Just as the briefing started, the chair next to me was finally occupied.

"Sorry, Lieutenant," Karlac, my copilot, whispered. He sought the most comfort possible that one could derive from a metal folding chair, propping his feet on the chair rung in front of him. "Better late than never," he spoke from the side of his mouth.

There was no time for my response as the room took on a hush. Colonel Terry made his way down the center aisle. I wondered when Terry slept because he looked bloated and top heavy, like a kid's bobble-head soldier. He stood at a podium on a makeshift metal stage with a Kelly green curtain tacked around the edge, giving it the appearance of a float. Colonel Terry was a big man with substantial fingers that gripped the edge of the podium as though glued in place. It wasn't even six in the morning, a mere seventy-five degrees outside, and already beads of sweat were forming on his brow. His shirt was wrinkled, and there were rings of perspiration stains under his arms, his tie loosened and uneven at the points.

He cleared his meaty throat. "Morning, gentlemen." He waited for the spectrum of murmurs in the assembly to subside. "No surprise to you, the war activities are intensifying and, as a result, the Army Air Corps, in conjunction with the RAF, has begun round-the-clock bombing schedules. Your missions will continue to involve orchestrated attacks by daylight while Britain's RAF will conduct their missions at night—same coordinated strategy, just more of it. The Allied ground war is surging forward and making steady progress, while the Allied air war is dominating." He knew to pause.

A few cheers went up in the room, and Terry patiently waited until the crowd quieted.

"World War I was a battle fought in trenches, gentlemen. World War II is being fought from above." He pointed toward the ceiling. "We're counting on heavy air defense, utilizing every Liberator and Flying Fortress available, ergo the decision months back to add missions by another nine and reduce crews to nine men. We believe this strategy will undoubtedly hasten the end of the war in Europe." He paused again to allow for the message to sink in. "Most of your missions have been to Munich and Berlin, an in-and-out full-team invasion in an effort to dismantle Hitler, get lucky, and catch him at a meeting. Didn't happen, and he has since gone on the move, so the targets and strategies have changed."

There was some groaning around the room, but to me the target didn't matter. I had confidence Leahy would hit it. My weighty pressure stemmed from getting us there and back unharmed. We had all heard the latest rumor that Adolf Hitler ordered all captured U.S. airmen to be shot on the spot. So far, we hadn't any knowledge of that order being carried out. Still, I didn't want my crew to ever be in that position, and eight men relied on me to safely deliver them while they did their jobs.

"As much as each one of us would be honored to take out Adolf Hitler permanently . . ."

The men vented more nervous energy toward the situation at hand. I saw it throughout the room, just as I recognized it among my crew and in myself on every mission—the jiggling of knees, the chain-smoking, the inappropriate jokes, and the cloistered outbursts—but less obvious was the simmering rage only held at bay by overwhelming fatigue and the stench of fear. If leaders didn't let their soldiers steam a bit, they'd have a powder keg on their hands, and no one knew how to moderate hundreds of men better than Terry.

The colonel continued after a considerable pause. "Gentlemen . . . gentlemen, please allow me to finish, I'll keep it brief." The room silenced again. "The primary targets we want to focus on are supply manufacturers and their routes. We need to sabotage the efforts of the Germans to construct the super highway under way. We will hit heavy on various rail stations, artery roads, and off-radar transport routes. We'll revisit several munitions factories and warehouses, all in an effort to reduce the enemy's access to supplies. Of course, as in the past few months, we will continue to hammer primary objectives: airfields, aircraft plants, tank factories, power plants, and fuel depots."

Hitler, with Benito Mussolini in his back pocket, devised the plan to engineer a vast stretch of roadway with a straight ground route from Germany through Austria and into Italy. The Germans were brilliant strategists and far superior in their technological advances at that point. American soldiers were at a real disadvantage, Europe not being familiar turf. Harnessing the B-17 in my own country was a challenge, but in foreign and enemy territory I had to be at the top of my game at all times, and demand the same of my crew if we were going to survive.

Without further words, Colonel Terry ceremoniously yanked back the black curtain, let go of the fabric, and stepped from the stage. As usual, it was met with gasps and mumblings, which quickly dissipated, as everyone tried to keep their outward emotions low, the typical premission jitters to a minimum. Lieutenant Colonel James F. Berry, commanding officer of the 323rd Bomb Squadron, made his way up to the wall map with his wooden pointer and began to give itineraries.

The changes that stood out on this particular day were formation related. Formation referred to a group of aircraft in flight, specifically arranged or positioned relative to one another, so they proceeded as a unit. Positions varied depending on the number of aircraft in the formation. Aircraft flying in a formation as the target was approached stayed close together, assuring the bomb loads would hit fast and heavy on their target. In addition, a tight formation was a formidable weapon, displaying a greater concentration of firepower when attacked by Luftwaffe fighter aircraft. When a hundred or so B-17s were in formation, it was certainly a sight to behold, whether from the air or from the ground.

On this mission, formations were smaller groupings, headed for more targets. My realist side couldn't help but think, divide and conquer; we'd be less of a threat in smaller groups. All in all, I was always relieved when the target didn't seem to involve killing random innocent people. We were so brainwashed by the military not to think about that aspect, and most tried not to, I assume. I knew it would probably take years for me to even broach the subject of the number of lives I had affected when this was all over.

The entire mission, as missions went, was a relatively short run of four hours each way as opposed to a long run of twice or more that length. Regardless, the intensity of the enemy resistance in the form of the fighters or flak, based on previous experiences, was the main theme of conversation around the room. Aside from the typical Munich targets, I saw Berlin, Schweinfurt, Stuttgart, Leipzig, Nuremberg, and Peenemünde. Intelligence had reported an underground facility near the town of Peenemünde in northeast Germany where scientists were developing a long-range ballistic rocket capable of reaching New York from the west coast of France. Peenemünde was a heavily targeted area.

Secondary targets were always designated in case weather obscured the original destination's target. Most missions involved lengthy flights over German-held territory and exposure to swarms of Luftwaffe fighters coupled with highly efficient antiaircraft guns, yet they had to happen if we were to put an end to this war.

"Shit," was all Karlac muttered as squadron names and targets were being called. *Priority Gal* was headed to north Munich rail yards on a southeastern approach—secondary target, Nuremberg. Flight crews were the originators of the acronym ET, which to us was the time spent in enemy territory. In hours, how long would we be in danger? Deep down, we knew we were always at risk for the entire assignment, even in the Quonset hut in Bassingbourn.

Without a doubt, the month of July 1944 had been one of the most traumatic periods in *Priority Gal's* battle career, having participated in twelve grueling missions over some of the most terrifying targets in Germany. Casualty counts of men and aircraft—

before, during, and after delivering their lethal cargo—were high. Too often that month, we watched as nine crew members without the opportunity to safely parachute vanished without a trace—a sad and haunting sight indeed.

"I need to find the guy filling in for Krusan," I told my lax copilot.

He stood, then stretched his back, and spoke midyawn. "So I'll meet you at the jeep."

I turned from him, convinced my copilot was deluded into believing his family wealth could save his life. I made my way to the side tables, where the navigators were picking up detailed instructions. Before I could even focus on any one navigator, someone came up from behind me.

"Lieutenant Supchak, sir?"

When I turned, Lieutenant Feinman stood like a mannequin, at attention, and gave a sharp salute the likes of which I hadn't seen since my training days. We shook hands. "At ease, Feinman." We made our way toward the exit. "I've heard some good things about you, so you better not let me down; you're filling some big shoes today."

We exited the rear of the Quonset hut.

"I'll do my best, sir, and with all due respect, you stole my line—I'm the one who should be saying I heard great things about you. I'm looking forward to flying a mission with someone with your combat knowledge and experience."

I grinned. A shame Krusan wasn't this polite, then I'd have the perfect combination. We made our way to the revved-up jeep waiting to drive us out to the airfield. I introduced Feinman to the other two offi-cers and would do the same thing when we met up with the rest of the crew.

My enlisted guys were already out with *Priority Gal,* doing the prep, and had been out there since four in the morning. They were experts at readying the bomber in top condition, and I had faith in their abilities, each and every mission. It was always music to my ears to hear: "*Gal's* ready, sir."

THREE

PRIORITY GAL'S CREW WAS ORIGINALLY ASSEMBLED at an air base near Salt Lake City, Utah, in February 1944. We consisted of four commissioned officers and six enlisted airmen: senior pilot, copilot, navigator, and bombardier were housed in the forward section of the bomber; and the flight crew chief, radioman, tail gunner, two waist gunners, and the ball turret gunner maintained the remaining two-thirds of the aircraft.

Intensive training began immediately upon check-in. Unabated education of preflight work was necessary to perform the duties as a flight team; each member was fully aware of his responsibilities in preparation for aerial warfare in an expedient timeframe. Two months later, in April 1944, we flew a brand-new B-17 and landed in Donegal Bay, Ireland, completing our first flight across the Atlantic. We left the christened B-17 behind, hitched a train through Scotland and reached Bassingbourn, England—just in time to be assigned to *Priority Gal* and briefed for our first mission over Germany.

Made in February 1944, *Priority Gal* was named after the original pilot who delivered her from Seattle, Washington, to Bassingbourn, a guy by the name of Pryor. Some pilots had the esteemed honor of naming their new bombers, and a symbol of that name was conspicuously painted on the nose section of the fuselage. It was in keeping with tradition perpetuated by flight and ground crews to display a personal pride in their flying machines. When the crew completed all its missions, the bomber was passed down, nose art and all, to a new crew. Most of the paintings were artistic, while others were humorous, if not graphic. Pinup girls seemed to be the most popular among the crews. Rumor had it that the picture of the girl on our B-17 had been a photo sent by a stateside friend to one of the original crew.

When *Priority Gal* was turned over to me, I guess one could say it was love at first flight. Our *Gal* was depicted as a stretching bathing beauty, a pinup girl, smiling and winking flirtatiously, a thought bubble saying, "Hurry back, guys." It was customary, before and after each mission, for the crew members to invariably reach up and give her a tender, meaningful pat on her backside, or other places, for luck. The guys smirked and laughed at the gesture, a male thing, I guess you could say, but it served a purpose, especially before a long combat mission. When a bomber was cited for some outstanding achievement, it was the painted figure that received the publicity. The nose art and small painted bombs were unique to each aircraft, and that visual told a very personal and heroic story. *Priority Gal* already was adorned with twenty-seven bombs just above her painting. My job was to tack on another thirty-five bombs before I could join Pryor's crew back in the states.

We didn't know when it would all be over or who would win, but the loyalty surrounding each bomber was likened to being part of a team, a team headed to a Super Bowl on each and every mission, except instead of a ring and an all-paid trip to an amusement park for the winning team, our reward was permission to live another day. Each and every guy in my crew was proud to be assigned to *Priority Gal*. We came to love our *Gal*, as we affectionately referred to her, and she held up her end of the deal on every mission so far.

The expansive airfield was situated twenty-five miles north of London near the village of Bassing-bourn. The base housed several hundred men endowed with the knowledge of all aspects of flight warfare. We flew over the English Channel on a regular basis, and with Cambridge University three miles east of the airfield, bombers frequently buzzed over the campus, sometimes low and loud with all four engines at full throttle for the students' benefits and cheers.

Priority Gal was named by the original pilot, Lt. Pryor, and was taken over by Lt. Henry Supchak and his crew in April 1944. The plane was built in Seattle, Washington, and accepted into inventory on February 17, 1944. The aircraft was a member of the 323rd Bomb Squadron, 91st Bomb Group of the Eighth Air Force and based at Bassingbourn, England. (*Gerry Asher*)

I had a healthy respect for my assignment as her command pilot. The B-17 was a massive aircraft, equipped with twelve powerful .50-caliber machine guns mounted strategically from the nose section to the tail. With four engines, the aircraft was capable of delivering two tons of destructive explosives to a target nearly a thousand miles away. It truly earned the reputation of being mighty.

In combat, I was no longer just a pilot. I was charged with all the duties of managing a crew and equipment. I was flying a ten-man weapon, responsible for safety and efficiency at all times of my crew, not just when we were flying and fighting, but for the full twenty-four hours of every day. I took my command very seriously.

I ran a tight ship and believed that practice made near perfect. Sure, I knew the guys bitched and groaned behind my back when I woke them in the middle of the night to practice drills, especially the bailout drills. There were so many situations that could arise, so we practiced at least twice a week. I tried to anticipate crises and train them to get through it as a team. That was my theoretical approach, although most times events arose and we learned after the fact, but that was okay too—we were just grateful we were alive to learn the lesson. What I did take away from all the preparation sessions was that my crew may have hemmed and hawed behind my back about my high expectations, but they always fully cooperated and never once said a negative word in my presence. They treated me with the utmost respect when face-to-face, and I took that as a positive.

We role-played scenarios of someone in the crew "losing it." We debated whose job it would be to step up and cover for a lost man. My crew knew what altitude to put the oxygen on and what to do when temperatures were below freezing. In an unpressurized aircraft, such as the B-17, an airman didn't necessarily know when the air was thinning, so he had to always be prepared. I relied on my crew chief, Sergeant Glenn Thomas, to ensure that the men in the rear of the fuselage—namely, the tail and waist

Lt. Henry Supchak's crew photographed in March 1944. Standing from left to right are: Sgt. Guy La Rocco, ball turret gunner; Sgt. Michael Hettler, radio operator/gunner; Sgt. Anthony Skorpik, waist gunner; Sgt. William Sheppard, tail gunner; Tech/Sgt. Glenn Thomas, flight crew chief and top turret gunner. Kneeling from left to right: Lt. Wilson Leahy, bombardier; Lt. Robert Krusan, navigator; Lt. John Karlac, copilot; Lt. Supchak, pilot. (*Author*)

gunners—were equipped with compressed oxygen and were dressed accordingly. Most of the time that involved leather and sheepskin from head to toe and gloves to guard against frostbite at our usual cruising altitudes of over twenty thousand feet.

If a crew member needed to relieve himself during a mission, there was a special "P-tube," but it was most inconvenient. We often avoided eating and drinking prior to a long mission for the obvious reasons. Regardless of what was happening to the individual crew member on a physiological level, he still had to remain vigilant to everything that was going on around him. We were always on constant alert, ready for attacks by Luftwaffe fighters, particularly the ruthless Messerschmitts, from anywhere and everywhere without warning. The goal was to be prepared and pray that neither mind nor body betrayed you.

By mid-May 1944, somewhere around our twelfth mission, U.S. crews were reduced to nine men, removing a waist gunner, so one airman handled the machine guns on both sides of the bomber. President Franklin D. Roosevelt justified the decision by adding additional bombers that needed crews. No one really knew the big picture, the real gains and losses.

It was also decided that thirty-five instead of twenty-five missions needed to be completed before returning stateside. As a "gift," if the crew completed thirty-four missions, the government credited it with the thirty-fifth. Allied politicos applauded our efforts on a regular basis, wanting us to be positive about the job we were performing on behalf of the world. The only reality I knew for certain was that every day several bombers didn't return to base after a mission, and lives were lost. Regardless of any political decisions, either well thought out or impulsive, I could only control my crew, and I was confident they were a well-trained, alert, and dependable group of brave men.

Some of the officers treated their crew as second-class citizens, but that wasn't my style. Completing the mission successfully was my goal, and my crew members knew that about me; we each had several air medals to prove it. In Europe, though, smack in the middle of a war zone, no one really cared how many medals you earned. The real question was: *Did you bring your boys safely home?* This being our thirty-third mission, I'd say, so far, so good. I really didn't know how success for a pilot was gauged during war other than the number of bombs painted on the nose of the bomber and the simple fact that you lived to talk about it.

FOUR

As if it were a spotlight from God, the sun lit the aluminum sides of the bombers, giving them an ethereal glow while they readied for takeoff. The side window of my cockpit was open just enough for me to pat the outer shell of the bomber, my way of saying good luck to the ole *Gal* painted below, before latching my window shut.

"Sir, sorry to interrupt your preflight, but the crew is not happy with another bombing mission to Munich." Crew Chief Thomas stood at attention behind me on the flight deck, a nervous guy, but for some strange reason it comforted me that he had just enough anxiety to make him perfect for his job. The man was all business and loyal as the day was long.

"I can't blame 'em, Sergeant, they know we're headed into a web of antiaircraft, not to mention fighter attacks. Hell, I'm not happy, either." I winked at Thomas, and his shoulders relaxed. "We all want to finish and go home, but until then, your job is to keep the men in line and make sure they're focused on the prize and not sitting around feeling sorry for themselves. Look how well you've done so far, thirty-two missions, Thomas, under pretty crummy conditions for the most part, yet your men have kept it together. That's something to be proud of, don't ya think?"

"Well, yes, thank you, sir. Can I say, with all due respect, sir?" He waited, so I nodded for him to go on. "I, myself, can't wait to get home, haven't seen my little girl since she was six months old." He bowed his head.

"I'm sure she's very proud of you. Is that all, Sergeant?" I needed for Thomas to stay focused, and his little anything back home wasn't going to help. "Get back to post and do what you do best."

"Yes, thank you, sir." He seemed relieved he didn't have to get emotional. With that, he stiffened and backed away to resume his post at the midsection of the bomb bay area.

I had to admit I wasn't just blowing smoke at Thomas. I, too, was a bit unnerved. All the black cloaked secrecy over the day's targets was ridiculous because the Germans already knew our strategy—they had spies everywhere. They knew the Eighth Air Force was returning, giving the Nazi's ample time and opportunity to reposition their guns and add more fighters in an effort to down as many B-17s and B-24s as possible. No one had any trouble visualizing what resistance the German welcoming committee would display. To make matters worse, I had a copilot who seemed bored with the war, and a pink-cheeked substitute navigator who was barely of shaving age.

At 0730, with all four engines humming in synchronized pitch, Karlac and I were given the green light from the control tower to take off. Within a few minutes, we lifted off the runway smoothly and began the climb to our rendezvous area at the predetermined altitude over the English Channel. This early, we allowed the Cambridge coeds to sleep in, while we stealthily took our place in a flight formation of a hundred other bombers from the 91st Bomb Group.

With all planes in position, the lead pilot issued a coded procedural message informing the rest of us in the formation that we were setting a direct course for Munich and would be climbing to an altitude of twenty-eight thousand feet. We acknowledged his final message for strict radio silence thereafter. If all went well, our formation, or whatever remained of it after the air battle over Munich, could expect to be back in England in seven hours, most of those over enemy territory.

"So, sir," Feinman asked me, "what was your most exciting mission so far? I myself would have loved to be a pilot, but I got a clubfoot. It's been repaired since I was in diapers, but they wouldn't let me in flight school."

"Well, Feinman," Leahy intervened, "they're idiots because the feet are the only part of the body you don't need to fly. Unless, of course, you're bailing out. In that scenario it doesn't matter if you have clubs or claws or suction cups—my all-time favorite—you're still up shit's creek." Leahy laughed into his headset. "Just joking, pal. You probably would have made a fine pilot. Get it, *Fine*—, Feinman."

Wilson Leahy, *Priority Gal's* bombadier, in 1944. (*Author*)

I was relieved the two of them were getting along, and I didn't end up with some young hotshot for a navigator. "Feinman, don't let Leahy corrupt you." So far, the newbie navigator had an easy go of it. It was a clear European morning, and I could have done this part of the route in my sleep. "Leahy can tell you some of our more interesting missions, I suppose. Carry on."

After that, I listened to Leahy reminisce from the nose of the plane, or the *greenhouse*, as he referred to it. My only regret was that I couldn't see the expression on Feinman's face.

"Here's a story that'll keep you up at night. We were returning from a mission, a short one, still mid-day, and we were close to base when the plane on our starboard side in the formation lost a wing, and the bomber just fell away. Everyone in the plane bailed out, and we watched as chutes opened, 1-2-3-4, and so on, but one airman, his chute didn't open, but what appeared to be the guy's laundry blew out of the chute pouch."

I couldn't help but cut in: "That's a helluva story to tell the new guy, Leahy!" I assumed Leahy would tell a harrowing story, but not that one. I didn't want a panicked novice giving me directions. "From that day forward, Feinman, I personally check each and every pack before takeoff—part of my preflight," I reassured the poor kid. "Trust is critical up here, but a functioning chute means surviving down there."

Leahy piped up: "Okay, Commander, what d'ya got? Tell us a positive war story." There was an insinuation of sarcasm when he said the word "positive."

"Don't be facetious, Leahy. There was one beautiful thing, as I recall, took my breath away, but unfortunately it's also on the day of my worst memory—D-Day." I paused just long enough for Feinman to react.

"*Priority Gal* participated in D-Day? Whoa, I am riding in a real piece of history! What was that like, flying the coast of France?"

"We're not talking about a honeymoon, Feinman, we're talking about my personal worst flying experience," I said, sounding maudlin on purpose. "For the ground soldiers who survived that day, it will invade their random thoughts for the rest of their lives.

Certainly will stay with me, and I wasn't even down on those beaches." We were quiet for a while.

"That beach scene certainly wasn't in the exotic vacation brochure the military gave me."

I had to smile at Leahy for bringing the conversation to a side light enough for the story to be told. I looked out my side of the bomber, then Karlac's window. The sky was blue and cloudless, an advantage for spotting those ubiquitous Messerschmitt fighters we'd soon be encountering. For the time being, it was quiet sailing in the armada.

FIVE

PROBABLY THE MOST SIGNIFICANT DATE IN THE war in Europe was June 6, 1944—D-Day, or decision day—when an immense Allied military force began its offensive by storming the Normandy coastline's many miles of beachfront, well fortified by the Germans, who fiercely fought the Allied invaders from Cherbourg to Calais. It was an unprecedented and well-coordinated maneuver using land, sea, and air forces in huge numbers. The hope was that this strategy would be a major turning point in the defeat of the German military machine.

On D-Day, *Priority Gal* was assigned to bomb German gun emplacements near the town of Saint-Lô, France, located twenty miles south of Omaha Beach. We were also responsible for destroying similar targets along Utah Beach in the Cherbourg

Peninsula. Juno, Sword, and Gold beaches near the Pas de Calais were the other assault areas assigned to the British and Canadian forces. *Priority Gal* was involved in bombing missions on June 2 and 5, and then back-to-back missions on D-Day.

On June 6, at approximately 0630, *Priority Gal's* flight path was directly over Omaha Beach as hundreds of landing craft were disembarking their cargoes of troops. The *Gal's* assigned altitude was low, because weather made for poor visibility, so at eight thousand feet we had a panoramic view of all the activity along the beach. It was spectacular and easily observed as far east and west as the eye could see. Another advantage to stormy weather over Normandy was that the German fighters couldn't fly that low without risk of killing their own soldiers and damaging their foothold.

It was obvious that day that the main objective was for these ground soldiers to get from their landing craft off the shoreline to relative safety at the base of the cliffs, where the enemy would be unable to get to them, as quickly as possible. If 20 percent made it to the cliffs, it was a lot. We knew those guys down there were barely out of high school. It was the saddest sight to behold—it looked like a bunch of dead ants strewn across miles of beachfront. With tens of thousands of soldiers missing in action during World War II, I was sure a good portion of that statistic related back to this day. There were so many men who never even made it out of the water. There wasn't a dry eye on the plane during that mission, and it was a silent and solemn return flight back to England. It's the stuff nightmares are made of.

The only encouraging thing that day was on our southern course to Saint-Lô. Atop of the cliffs, we caught sight of thousands of deflated parachutes strewn over a massive area, left behind by Allied paratroopers, who discretely landed sometime during the very early hours of that morning. That was a beautiful thing to see. Here it was June, and the ground looked covered in snow. This memory was so significant because it was the only positive image I'd ever experienced during a mission.

Karlac piped in for the first time all morning. "The other really sorry mission was the one with Hettler, poor bastard. Sergeant Michael Hettler was our radioman, the only guy on any of our missions so far who got seriously injured," Karlac explained to Feinman. "He stayed to himself for the most part, carried that violin around with him everywhere. He even brought it on all the missions, stowed it at his feet under his desk. If we had an excessively long mission, he'd pluck songs from the instrument, even when strings broke and he had no way of replacing them in a war zone. No one seemed to mind, it was comforting in a way. Sometimes late at night you could hear him gently plucking some familiar tune. He loved his violin, had lessons as a kid until the Depression hit. It didn't matter to him, though. He called his violin *Friend*, and he swore it saved his sanity.

Lt. Henry Supchak, right, reviewing premission procedures with flight crew chief Sgt. Glenn Thomas, left, and radio operator Sgt. Michael Hettler, center. (*Author*)

"Somewhere around our twentieth mission, an antiaircraft bullet came up through the bottom of the bomber and tore into his violin satchel, then traveled through his wooden radio desk, sending more than a thousand slivers of wood from the desk into the right side of his face. The violin bow had been snapped in two but had slowed down the speed and diverted the bullet in a right angle, otherwise it would have come straight up the center of the desk and hit Hettler in the throat, killing him instantly."

The look on Feinman's face had to be priceless after Karlac's story, especially because Feinman was sitting at a similar wooden desk in the greenhouse. After several brief stories on the various horrors of air combat, we all seemed to fall into a complacent silence. Although the rhythmic thrum of the four engines and the vibrations of the bomber lent themselves to relaxation, I knew we were all too busy contemplating what lay ahead. Adrenaline played a leading role in World War II.

SIX

"LET'S GET READY FOR BUSINESS." LEAHY GAVE the "twenty minutes from target" signal, and the crew assumed combat positions. So far, we hadn't encountered any bogie run-ins. Unfortunately, there had yet to be a mission without air-to-air attacks.

Karlac stood from his post and communicated with the crew chief that we were to "man up," which was the signal to ready his gunners. I had to give Karlac credit for his uncanny ability to do the bare minimum. He was fairly quiet and mild mannered for the most part, but for whatever reason he seemed to rub the crew the wrong way. They found him snobbish and standoffish. I had nothing against the guy. He did his job, but I knew in an emergency situation it had always been Krusan and Leahy who took leadership roles. A group of men thrown together in the middle of a war zone made for strange bedfellows. War changed people, and I needed the men to get along; camaraderie among the crew made them easier to manage.

The southeastern course to Munich took us over well-protected German strongholds like Frankfurt, Mainz, Stuttgart, and Regensburg. Just after Karlac strapped himself back into the copilot seat, we began to get shot at from the ground. Antiaircraft pummeled several bombers in the armada, and the B-17 to our left exploded in midair and fell away. I had to press on to the target; we were trained to think forward, not to think about those nine men who just widowed and orphaned their families. That's what we did, but it only got us so far. We ran through some heavy flak, but avoided any direct hits on our way in to Munich.

When *Priority Gal* began to hit thick, dark storms of exploding flak shells, it got dicey. The accuracy of some German antiaircraft gunners was phenomenal. We knew that when German fighter attacks ceased and the planes began getting the hell out of dodge, it was a signal that they didn't want to get taken out by friendly antiaircraft fire about to start from below. This went back and forth like a well-orchestrated dance between tarantulas: one will inevitably go down. Our only recourse on any mission was to hit the target and get beyond their range as quickly as possible while staying in formation as assigned.

Priority Gal, top, in its natural metal finish, in formation with *Sweet 17–The Spirit of St. Louis,* right, and *Nine O Nine,* in camouflage paint in center. The bomb bay doors are open. Both *Sweet 17* and *Nine O Nine* survived the war, the latter flying a remarkable 140 missions. The 91st Bomb Group used a capital letter A within a triangle for its insignia. (*Gerry Asher*)

We approached the target area above Germany, and Lieutenant Leahy took over the controls. He quickly and efficiently conducted his routine of operating the bombing equipment. Before he was able to release the bomb bay doors, an 88mm flak shell ripped through the number four engine and exploded about fifty feet above us, showering the bomber in a hailstorm of debris.

"Damn it!" I heard Leahy shout. "And now for the bad news: Bogie, two o'clock high!"

"Handle it, men, I got a burning engine!" I took back the controls and knew Leahy would step up to the task.

Through the headset, I heard him yell like a gym teacher: "Gunners! Thomas, Sheppard, Skorpik, Rocco, look alive, men!" I knew my gunners could ward off the best of the Me-109s a few at a time, but as we closed in on target Munich, it would only get worse. From where I sat I visually assessed the smoking starboard engine. Sergeant Kenneth Taylor, the radioman who took over after Hettler, didn't have a whole lot to do at that point, so I ordered him to watch out the starboard side for damage. He had a view of the rear of the wing, being behind the cockpit. I was certain for the remainder of the mission we'd be singled out as a target, like a bleeding body in a pool of sharks.

"Feather the blades, Karlac! Then get the backend crew ready!" I gave a direct order to my copilot. Karlac quickly tried to stop the propeller from rotating in an effort to avoid resistance, but it wouldn't respond. The flak shell undoubtedly damaged its mechanism.

"More flames, sir, starboard," a befuddled Karlac reported from his side of the bomber.

"Hit the fire extinguisher again!" I ordered, gesturing to the control panel where the emergency tabs were located. If the fire penetrated the engine and the fuel tanks, the plane would explode.

Karlac hit the number four extinguisher tab and the flame went out, leaving a trail of dark smoke. If visibility became an issue for my wingmen on that side, I'd be given an order to pull out of formation. But so far we were cleared to stay with the armada, but that didn't allay my mounting anxiety. Unabated conjecture reigned, and I knew we were flying on a wing and a prayer.

When Leahy announced he had the target in the crosshairs, Karlac headed to the back of the bomber to assess the situation. Leahy had the gears, and following "Bombs away!" the entire formation began a U-turn to the right, setting a direct course back to England. Controls back in my hands, with three engines functioning satisfactorily, I was able to maintain our altitude and flight position in the formation. Karlac's job, when he returned to his seat, was to keep a very close watch on engine four.

"That'll put some hair on your chest, Feinman, won't it?" Leahy teased when he returned to the greenhouse after checking the bomb bay.

Feinman didn't respond. With only three missions under his belt, his experience was limited. I had grown accustomed to the longstanding solidarity between Leahy and Krusan. They were each other's straight man, but Feinman had no history with *Priority Gal*, and he had to be a bit affected by the surrounding events. He was just a kid.

"No sign of fire, just a few intermittent sparks and increasing smoke," Karlac reported every so often.

Priority Gal was managing to hold her own. A little shot up, but she had successfully completed her thirty-third and next to last mission. As always, I needed to get us safely back to England. Then one more mission after that, and in less than a month *Priority Gal* and her crew would be home free.

SEVEN

O N THE OUTSKIRTS OF MUNICH, THE FORMATION was bombarded again from below with more antiaircraft missiles. My number three engine was hit by a shell that tore a huge hole in its nacelle section. This one exploded mere feet above us, like a thunderclap, sending shards of metal smashing against the bomber. A shell fragment about a half inch in diameter and two inches in length found a weak seam in the cockpit's ceiling and wedged into my thigh just above my right knee.

"*Ughghgh!*" I yelled. "Son of a bitch!" I grabbed my thigh, and pain shot down to my toes. I knew it was in there deep, but I also knew to leave it there, where it served as a cork.

"Shit, sir, you okay?" Karlac inquired and sounded concerned. "How can I help?"

"Negative, Lieutenant." There were too many other things to worry about. "I'll live." When those last two words escaped my mouth, I hoped I hadn't jinxed myself.

"Damn it, we lost engine number three," Karlac reported, but I didn't need him to tell me because I saw my instruments going haywire in their attempt to compensate and readjust. I leaned to see out the right window for the hundredth time that flight. Sparks were spewing from both engines' outtakes.

I radioed the lead plane that we were aborting the formation and then gave a signal to my left wingman. I received the thumbs-up from his copilot. The mishap would immediately be reported to base by the lead pilot.

"I'm pulling from formation, zero explanation necessary at this point. Feinman, Leahy, you with me?" I queried.

"Yo, boss, actually we're in front of you." Leahy, always the smart-ass, which continually endeared him to me.

"Sir, yes, sir." Feinman muttered, as if surrendering to a firing squad. I knew he was nervous as all get out because I was, and I had years of experience over the kid.

"Put our course west to Switzerland. It's the closest neutral border." I figured Leahy would tell me if Feinman had ceased to function. "We're aiming for Lake Constance."

"A water landing, sir?" Karlac cut in, visibly disturbed for the first time that morning. "You sure that's the way to go here?"

"Lieutenant, we have a burning plane, it's the only way." I turned my attention to the greenhouse. "Feinman, where we at?"

"Sir, sorry, I took us a little too far south, but we are now on a western route to Switzerland. To the lake, sir, the one you requested," Feinman reported in a voice barely audible.

I had to be gingerly in what I said; he was still in my charge, and perhaps this was a good learning moment for the youngster. "How far south, Feinman?"

"Well, maybe thirty miles, sir."

"The problem for us in this situation, Lieutenant Feinman, is we are rapidly losing altitude and don't have room for thirty-mile mistakes." No sense belaboring the point. Thirty miles out of the way meant sixty miles total after recovery. Not good.

"No, sir, um . . . I mean . . . yes, sir."

"Head in the game, Feinman."

The crew chief made his way to the cockpit. "Sir, Rocco is reporting smoke and flames from both engines. He says we're out of formation, sir? Oh, God, your knee is bleeding."

"Lieutenant Karlac?" I balled my fists in anger but did my level best not to punch my copilot in the face. "I told you to ready the men in the back, meaning get Rocco's ass out of the ball ASAP!" I threw my arms up in exasperation and turned to my crew chief. "For Christ's sake, Sergeant Thomas, get back to your post, get Rocco the hell out of the ball, and update your crew that we have aborted formation because both right engines are on fire. Have the men get their chutes on!"

"We're bailing?!" Thomas sounded panicked.

"Thomas, listen to me because I'm only explaining this once. We have a plane that needs four engines to fly straight; we have two dead on one side. You do the math. We've practiced this routine, and you're responsible for those guys back there. Remember, Thomas, they're your men."

The poor guy awkwardly saluted me, then his eyes glanced down to my bloodied leg. He stiffened his jaw and turned from the cockpit. I was touched by his concern for my injury, and it felt like what I imagined a searing-hot fireplace poker would feel like, but there was no time for fretting and reassurances. As the senior officer, it was my duty to empower my crew chief, and I knew Thomas would carry out my order, as if he were a robot.

When I turned my attention back to the copilot, he had somewhat redeemed himself by successfully feathering the propeller in engine number three. It stopped rotating, eliminating some immediate issues involved in controlling the plane. "Alright, Karlac, good work."

With two disabled engines spewing smoke and sparks, I knew the situation was grave. If we were

A B-17 of the 91st Bomb Group going down over Germany. The dark specks to the left of the wing and above the horizontal stabilizer at the top are two crew members who have bailed out. (*USAF*)

lucky enough to land in Switzerland, we would still be taken captive, albeit a far better situation than dropping into Hitler's Austria directly below us.

"Uh, yeah, John. Doesn't look like we're making it back anytime soon, headed to the Swiss border, possible water landing. Can you stop by the post exchange and get my dry cleaning and laund—?"

Incredulous, I looked to my right to find my copilot holding a live handset connecting him back to base. I slapped the handset from his palm. "Are you out of your mind, Karlac? Why would you break radio silence? Of all the goddamn times! Why not rent a banner announcing where we are to the Germans?" I was stunned at the jeopardy my copilot had placed us in at that moment. Granted, we were crippled, but the Germans relished the idea of knocking all of us right out of the sky and into enemy borders.

No sooner had Karlac sheepishly replaced his handheld when Leahy yelled, "Me-109, twelve o'clock high!" I heard several shots fired from the nose guns as the German fighter issued his own share of wild pops before disappearing from sight. "Christ, that was close! Goon must have run out of ammo or figures we're going down anyway, so why risk his own neck wasting bullets? He's got our number; he'll get credit for the hit." My bombardier sounded nervous, something I'd believed foreign to his personality. Then again, we were never this badly injured.

I knew it was only a matter of minutes before more German fighter reinforcements attacked. We were defenseless—sitting ducks on our own with very little hope of reaching Switzerland as we continued to lose altitude.

"We have some mountain ranges ahead we will not make it over, sir," Feinman sounded, as if he were crying. "It has been a pleasure flying with you and I—"

"—Shut up, Feinman! You can kiss his ass on the ground, but for now you need to get your eyes on the compass!" Leahy interceded. He'd handle Feinman.

Meanwhile, I was preoccupied by the mountain range, the Austrian Alps, likely one of the largest in the world, looming just ahead of us. As Feinman confirmed, I knew we would never make it over them.

I gave the order to Karlac to tell Thomas to line up for bailout. As they stood by for my order to jump, a flak battery of six guns near Innsbruck, Austria, shot at us and did enough damage to partially dislocate *Priority Gal*'s right wing.

"Karlac, Leahy, Feinman! Get your chutes on and prepare to bail, that's an order!"

"I'm sticking around, sir, where you fly, I fly." Leahy was sincere. "Besides, a nice refreshing swim in Lake Constance sounds appealing."

"Me, too, sir," Feinman piped up as he stuck his head up through the dome at the roof of the greenhouse so I could see the loyalty on his young face. He gave the thumbs-up signal.

"Change of plans, men. We're not making any lake in Switzerland on this vacation. The right wing is hanging by a thread, so get the hell out of the plane unless you want to go down with her. I'm giving you jackos an order!"

Without being told twice, Karlac had made his way down to the greenhouse, and I was alone in the cockpit. I yelled back to my crew chief, "Thomas, how many of your guys left?!"

He was leaning partway into the cockpit. "Sir, no one's jumped yet. Sergeant Rocco's frozen in the hatch."

Of all the soldiers, the brave little braggadocio ball turret gunner from Brooklyn was the last one I expected to lose it. I lifted my right boot and gave the pantomime of kicking someone's ass out of the plane, then winced when a bolt of pain ripped through my leg.

Thomas, doing just that, succeeded in getting his men out and then himself. Next went the three officers in the nose at my signal. Leahy, the last to bail, stuck his head in the dome of the greenhouse before jumping and saluted me. "See you on the other side, Lieutenant!" Then he was gone.

I was alone, and *Priority Gal* was dying.

PART TWO

The Boy

EIGHT

ANDER HAAS HAD NO WAY OF KNOWING HIS LIFE was moments away from being changed forever. He was only six and too busy thinking that ever since he heard of the führer, life on his family's farm was different. If it weren't for the war, Ander would have been in school down in the village, just like his sisters.

Instead, he spent hours shepherding hairy animals in the thorny brush outside his family's sheepshearing hut nestled high in the Austrian Alps. On a decent morning Ander wrangled eight sheep at best, because they weighed more than he did. It was worse in the afternoon when he had to bundle the coarse wool into burlap sacks. "The sheep were ornery today, just like Ander," he sometimes overheard his aunt tell his mum.

In summer, when temperatures choked the valley, his aunt allowed him to relax a spell down in the ravine, where crisp, fresh water ran from an ancient glacier. He loved to sit on the cold smooth stones while the icy stream raced beneath him. Sometimes, at the end of the day, when the evening fell cool, he and Aunt Julia would sit side by side on the weather-beaten split-rail fence and watch the wild goats frolic in the ravine waters as the sun faded over the far side of the mountains. The evening sky was always beautiful, even on cloudy days. All things considered, though, Ander ached for his life to return to the way it was before the war.

World War II had taken its toll on the Haas family. Before the SS soldiers took over their village, the Haas family had three sheep farms, but now the whole family lived on one farm, overcrowded with ten people. Ander's papa handled most of the shearing work until he was sent to Germany to fight in the war. Ander missed his papa so much it hurt, and he didn't know if he'd ever see him again. His mum explained the family needed to be supportive of the Reich, but Ander heard a sharp edge in her voice when she said it.

Every evening, when it was time to go back to the village, his aunt drove the rusted-out truck with the day's shearings down the rocky terrain to the SS outpost. Ander got to ride on the bundles in back, and he secretly loved that part; the bumpy downhill ride felt as if a gentle giant were carrying him home. The

soldiers who greeted them
when he and his aunt
returned with the truck and
wool acted silly around his
aunt, pushing and chiding
each other, but she paid them
no mind. She gracefully
accepted the daily paper
money along with the food
rations they gave her in
exchange for the wool, but
she never accepted the soldiers' offers to drop Ander
and her at their farm. He

Ander Haas as a toddler,
with his feet in his father's
shoes. (*Ander Haas*)

wished she would say *yes* just once because his legs
always ached on that walk back home. Often he was
so tired he didn't eat supper. He'd go to bed and fall
asleep to the sounds of his sisters' giggles from the
kitchen, and he imagined someday he'd be a soldier
like the ones from the outpost, and then he'd get to
boss girls around.

Some days in the Alps, Ander could see the war
taking place. He knew in Innsbruck there were big
guns that came up from the ground when enemy
planes tried to make it to Switzerland. He heard a few
soldiers talking about it once; they thought he was
too young to understand as they spoke about death.
Ander knew about guns and about death. All the soldiers carried guns, big ones. On clear days he had
seen the grey-and-black puffs of smoke rising in the

distance. The very idea of ground guns piqued Ander's curiosity. Once, Ander's father was forced to shoot an infirm sheep, and when Ander heard the shot from inside the shearing hut, it made him cry. Afterward, his papa held Ander close in his arms and kissed the top of his head and told him that if he were to be of the Reich someday, he had to be very brave, that sometimes life was sad.

This day was shaping up to be a scorcher, his aunt had said that morning over cheese, sweet pickles, and smoked ham as sunlight made its way through the farmhouse's kitchen window. His mum cut the sleeves off his shirt and gave him a salt tablet before he set out with Aunt Julia. Up at the shearing hut under the glaring sun, his aunt let him roll his knickers above his knees and his socks down to the tops of his shoes.

He was trying to shepherd and rope his third sheep of the morning, pathetically luring it with a piece of cheese, and he knew if his aunt found out he was wasting food, he would be punished. He had reasoned it was *his* cheese, so not having it didn't make anyone else's tummy rumble but his own. Ander felt sorry for the sheep; it was as if they thought they would be slaughtered and didn't realize his aunt just wanted to give them a haircut.

So there Ander was, squatting in the gravel along the hiking path, making dumb kissing noises to the plump, hairy animal ignoring him when he heard a roaring sound coming from the ridge up near the glacier. He felt it, more than anything. The vibrations and sound grew by the second until they seemed to split the sky. Ander looked up from the brush and saw the strangest sight—what appeared to be a massive dark bird wavering in the hot air like a mirage.

It finally occurred to Ander that a burning airplane was headed directly toward his village. It was a warplane, like the ones he saw in his sister's schoolbook, but something was terribly wrong with this plane. He turned to run and get his aunt, but she was already headed down the path. Her mouth was open like she was trying to say something, but the words were stuck, and this scared Ander a little because his aunt always had something to say.

"Wird es zusammenstoßen?" (Is it going to crash?) Ander asked, but she never answered; she had fallen to her knees and had begun to pray. The shepherd boy didn't know what to do, so he knelt as well. When he looked back at the midday sky, he watched as the huge lumbering plane strangely made a sudden sharp turn and traveled in the opposite direction of the village. The plane appeared to gather speed, then it tipped to the right and swayed before being lifted by an updraft. It wasn't going to crash into the village after all, but instead was headed into the side of the nearby mountain. Ander heard his aunt's screams to get down on the ground, but he was frozen in fascination by the monstrous fiery beast barreling straight toward him.

Then Ander saw something else he'd only seen in pictures. At first it looked like a package or a bomb had dropped from the plane, but then a white puff spread out and billowed, jerking the thing upward. It wasn't a thing at all, but a person slowly drifting down toward the freshly thatched pasture at the base of the mountain. A man was inside that burning plane, and he had steered it away from Ander's village. This man had to be one of the good guys for certain—maybe it was his papa.

The noise grew louder, and the enormity of the plane nearly upon them must have blocked Aunt Julia's screams because she shoved Ander to the ground right there in the prickly brush and covered him with her own body. Ander tried to tell her they'd be okay. His aunt didn't need to worry. It was one of the good guys, but she didn't hear him over the noise.

Just as Ander was about to squirm in protest because she was hurting him, a daunting, dark shadow with choking smoke enveloped them, and flying red-hot sparks lit blades of dried brush all around them as the crippled plane passed just meters overhead. Ander thought his ears would rupture; his skin burned and his eyes watered. The last thing he saw was the bright flash of white after the plane ripped through the split-rail fence and crashed head-on into the ravine. A deafening explosion followed, sending boulders and fireballs of molten metal in all directions, obliterating the shearing hut and everything else along the way.

NINE

"*Für Sie ist der Krieg vorbei.*"

I landed on a soft, grassy knoll—quite scenic, actually. Even though I had a nail-like projectile jutting from my right thigh and a wrenched lower back, I managed to stay afoot. Through dazed thoughts, from behind I heard the woman's voice again.

"*Für Sie ist der Krieg vorbei.*"

I turned cautiously, stumbling a bit around the cords of my chute. She was behind me, dressed from head to toe in black, just a pale round face, skin crocheted with age and worry. She smiled a toothless grin, and in perfect English she whispered in a soft, sweet voice something I would never forget: "For you, son, the war is over."

The sound of fierce growling made me snap to and turn back around. I was suddenly surrounded by four snarling German shepherd dogs, and I instinctively drew back toward where the woman stood, but she was gone. Four men in SS uniforms came up and yelled for the dogs to heel, and then one soldier aggressively shoved me. In broken English he ordered me to pick up my chute and start walking.

A small crowd of villagers were making their way toward the spectacle that was me. I had heard rumors that townspeople forced to observe German rule could be very nasty. They were resentful, stuck at ground zero in a world war zone, their land taken from them—it made sense. Usually they threatened and cursed the captives, sometimes even took shots at them, which made me very apprehensive. But all I witnessed that day were their wide-eyed stares, not mean glares yet not friendly, either—almost curious. I was much less concerned about the throng of local onlookers than I was about the soldier poking me in the back with his gun and yelling at me in German what I assumed to mean "Move it!"

After about a two-mile walk along a gravel road in a town with a sign bearing the word *Neustift*—the village I saw through the nose of my bomber—I was bleary and weak but consumed with concern about the outcome of the rest of my crew. If they survived the bailout, they were probably picked up by SS troops as well, but not knowing was the worst part. Hundreds of Austrian civilians lined the streets to watch the spectacle of my capture and imprisonment.

The Neustift area in the early 1940s showing one of the outlying estates opposite of the main town and ravine where *Priority Gal* crashed. Ander Haas and his aunt worked on the mountain in the foreground. (*Ander Haas*)

Finally we reached the German outpost where the SS officers were stationed. I was surprised they didn't waste any time interrogating me. In the office of the post's commander—*Hauptmann* (Captain) Metcalf, or at least that's what his wooden desk plate read—sat a large man, toothpick sticking through his thin lips, a man I judged to be about forty years of age. The captain spoke flawless American English, and in a formal military manner asked the usual questions about my background, to which I was obligated to give the usual response. Name, rank, serial number. Interestingly enough, I probably knew less than what the Germans already knew. We weren't privileged to know future strategies, only rumors and base scuttlebutt, if you will.

Frustrated I wasn't caving in to his menacing presence, he left me alone in the room. I sat in a wooden chair, unshackled, but didn't dare think about running. He returned a few minutes later and switched tactics.

"So you were raised in Nanticoke? Your mother, Lola, is that her name? Is she a secretary?" In a voice carrying more of a city-boy accent, he recited the names of all my family members. Then he claimed for the last fifteen years he had lived in Chicago, where he worked as a taxicab driver. When war broke out in his native country, he was obligated to return to Germany, where he was to serve as command for the eastern border patrol of Austria. He claimed he was specifically chosen because his English was decent.

When the war ended, he would head back to Chicago and resume his employ as a cab driver, a job he claimed to enjoy immensely. There is no doubt in my mind he was telling me the truth about his past, but I knew his loyalties lay with Germany, regardless of his love for the United States; for now, I was the enemy and his prisoner. I was mindful of rumors of airmen shot down and captured and then executed. So far, I was still alive, but for how long I didn't know.

Sometime in the late afternoon, after Metcalf had punched me in the gut a few times and roughed me up, all the while bragging about the lunch he had enjoyed that day of kartoffel, sauerbraten, and Wiener schnitzel, he quit. His final act was yanking the shrapnel from my leg without warning, tucking it neatly into my flight suit pocket, patting it as if it were a special gift, then taking lighter fluid and squeezing it into the open wound. I don't remember a worse pain; the shrapnel going into my thigh hadn't hurt nearly as much.

I was locked in a dark cell in the outpost. The walls were painted red, and there was a red bulb burning in a light socket several feet above me. A solid door on one side of the cell was opposite a rectangle of bright light shining through a hole the size and shape of a loaf of bread cut in the upper portion of the wall. I knew it was sunlight coming through, but barely able to bend my right leg, there was no way I could stand to look out. The benzene cauterized the bleeding, but the pain remained excruciating. Survival was now my only goal, water being the first essential I knew I couldn't live without. Although it seemed like days ago, I thought about my breakfast that morning. I had never before eaten three eggs and doubled up on everything else. I never wanted to be stuck at twenty-eight thousand feet with full lower intestines, but somehow that morning I ate large. I convinced myself there was no way I could be hungry yet. I guess it worked. I would never have imagined my bruised, battered, and dehydrated body could have succumbed to sleep. But somehow a tidal wave of fatigue overcame me, and I temporarily gave into it, only to be brought back to reality at some point—when light no longer shone through the hole in the wall, but a face did.

TEN

"Psst, sir." Ander wanted to get the man's attention before one of the SS soldiers spotted him. He stood on tiptoes on a wooden crate he found tossed behind the rubbish containers. Unfortunately, he only made out the ceiling with the odd red bulb. He heard no sound or movement from inside the cell. Aunt Julia was doing a great job of distracting the guards, an act he had never seen her do before, and it looked strange and silly.

"Psst, sir, *Ich habe etwas Wasser und Käse, auch.*" (I have some water and cheese and bread, too.) Ander couldn't tell from this vantage point if the man was still alive in the cell. When he and Aunt Julia showed up burned and upset, the soldiers were quite forthcoming with information about the American pilot they held captive in the room with the red light.

Earlier in the day—a day cut short of work when the plane crashed so close it leveled their hut and destroyed the old truck—Aunt Julia and Ander had to walk all the way down the mountain, burns and all. The burns were minor, just a small one on Ander's leg and another on his forearm, nothing a little salve wouldn't take care of, his aunt had reassured him when he cried.

Aunt Julia didn't seem to mind her burns or the walk down the mountain, for that matter; she laughed and hugged Ander all the way to the pasture. She kept saying the man that fell out of that plane had saved their village. He had turned the plane away, and she wanted to be sure he was safe.

By the time they reached the lower trail that led to the pasture, they saw a large crowd of villagers dispersing. There was no sign of the man with the white parachute. Aunt Julia had stopped laughing then. She told Ander that the SS soldiers must have taken him—the man must be the enemy. Ander didn't understand what she was saying. Wasn't he one of the good guys? Of course he was good, she kept repeating, and she was determined to know what happened to the man. Aunt Julia carried Ander the rest of the way back to the village. They bypassed the outpost this time and went straight home.

After a long walk back to the farmhouse, followed by wordy explanations to Ander's mum of what had occurred and his wound treatment, Aunt Julia had hatched a plan and she needed Ander's help to make it happen. After dinner, instead of going for a walk as they sometimes did, Ander and his aunt walked to the outpost.

They arrived at the outpost, Aunt Julia looking disheveled, and when she showed her small arm burns to the soldiers, they fell all over themselves to assist. While she explained about the exploding plane and the ruined truck, the soldiers were lost in her world, and Ander went to work.

After sneaking past the scene his aunt was making, he made his way to the far side of the building, where the soldiers held prisoners. The food and water package had to be given to the man—those were his instructions. Now he found himself atop a crate, and at first all he saw was the red ceiling; then, while Ander was on tiptoes for a better view, a man's bruised and bloodied face appeared in the opening, startling Ander so much he nearly fell backward off his perch.

The man was in bad shape. His face was pinched in a pained expression as he peered out at Ander from his cell. Ander figured his face must have been injured when he fell to the ground from the plane. Still, the man had kind eyes and a warm smile, just like Ander's papa. Ander tried to tell the man *danke* (thank you) for what he had done; his family was very grateful. He wanted the man to know he was sorry the soldiers took him prisoner, but Ander heard his Aunt Julia coughing, and he knew it was his signal to hurry up.

Ander handed the wrapped package through the small opening in the wall and watched for a moment while the man untied the string and tore open the brown paper: a pickle jar of water with a side of bread and cheese. Ander had never seen anyone drink and eat so fast, and his mum would say it was bad table manners if Ander behaved that way, but this time it was okay because the man was very hungry and thirsty. The man handed Ander back the paper and the jar and wiped his mouth on his dirty sleeve.

The man kept saying the words "thank you, thank you." Ander didn't understand. When Aunt Julia coughed for the third time, he jumped from the crate, tossed it behind the rubbish, and ran to where his aunt stood waiting. Ander knew if he wanted to come back and visit the American, he just couldn't get caught.

ELEVEN

THE BOY SAVED MY LIFE. IT WAS THAT SIMPLE.
Who was he? I had no idea. For three days I
roasted in that cell, and at night the boy came with
fresh food and water. We talked, though neither
understood each other. All I knew was this dark-
haired kid was not my enemy; he was kind and clever.
Under the glow of the red bulb, I wondered whether
the rest of my life would be lived in that very cell. If
so, I rationalized, at least I had the boy.

I knew there were adults behind the boy's sneaky
antics. At one point I thought I caught a glimpse of a
beautiful young female—an aunt or older sister to the
boy, too young for his mother. These innocent people
were risking their lives to help me. How could I ever
thank them? If I died in that cell, I reasoned, the kind
boy and young woman would be my last memory.

Every so often the door would open, and the guard would ask if I had anything to say besides name, rank, and serial number. When I shook my head, he'd leave a can of dirty water and lock the door again. Sleep came and went, and I still felt exhausted. I spent most of my time, which was all I had, learning to walk again. The cell was small, maybe seven by seven, so in an hour I could traverse the room several hundred times, each pacing session outdoing the previous one. My leg was getting stronger, I supposed, or maybe it wasn't as stiff since the shrapnel had been brutally yanked out—that had only been two or three days ago, yet it seemed like a lifetime had passed. I understood how a person could go insane alone in an empty red room. I could only assume that was the Germans' strategy.

No matter how many times the Nazis came in to interrogate me, I remained quiet. Instead of growing weaker, somehow I became more brazen, asking my terrorizers questions about my crew. This got me nothing but a kick to the ribs, and though my spirit wasn't broken, I knew I still had a very long and difficult journey ahead.

Crying my way to dehydration was not an option, but I felt a constant lump in my throat when I thought about my family back home. How difficult it must have been for my parents when the government officials showed up at their home to inform them that their son was missing in action—that his plane had gone down in enemy territory. When I first told my folks I was joining the war effort just after Pearl Harbor, they were not thrilled at the decision but gave me their blessings anyway. Their worst nightmare was probably happening at that very moment on the other side of the world: their only son was shot down over enemy territory and is reported missing in action.

Based on the number of visits from the boy, I knew I had been locked in that cell for three days. When the door was finally opened for good, the guards hoisted me up from my slumped position on the floor. I feigned pain and stiffness in my leg and back, but the truth was that I had paced enough to strengthen my back, and lessen the pain and swelling in my knee a bit. The food, water, and exercise had restored some fragment of wellness. The worst feeling just then was behind my eyes. I had tremendous interocular pain because of my pupils' eagerness to adjust to the white light from the corridor. The guards dragged me down a long hallway, and once again my fate was in question. Was this the end for me?

From a side hallway, *Hauptmann* Metcalf appeared. The guards stopped and let go of me. I was able to get my feet under me and hold my own. Metcalf stood inches from my face, toothpick dangling from his lower lip. His sour breath topped by stale cigarette smell placed the time as after lunch. "Well, well, well, Lieutenant. When you get to wherever it is that you're going, you will look back on these past few days as a vacation." He smiled.

I remained stoic, tightening the muscles in my gut in anticipation of a blow. Metcalf leaned against the wall and cocked his head. "I admire your loyalty, but eventually you will have to accept the inevitable." He turned to recede back down the dark, narrow hall from which he had emerged, then hesitated and turned back. *Here it comes*, I figured. "If you ever get back to the states and find yourself in Chicago," he winked, "look me up." Then, with a throaty laugh, *Hauptmann* Metcalf disappeared from my life.

The guards nudged me further to the end of the bright corridor. I was forced through a doorway and down a dark flight of stairs into some sort of basement. I couldn't make out anything, and my eyes were wreaking havoc with the sudden and harsh changes in lighting. There was a metal door at the bottom of the cement steps, and we stood in front of it for several seconds while the guard fumbled through a ring of keys. His cohort with the gun at my back whistled the American national anthem. It was a rather poor rendition, and they laughed mockingly. Their derogatory manner toward my country was as bothersome as any disparaging comments they had thrown at me over the past few days. I felt powerless.

"Ah!" the guard exclaimed and keyed the bolt on the door frame. We all knew about the death chambers, and I had to wonder if this was one of those. I was shoved into a dark, dank room, and the door was bolted behind me. The guards were gone, but someone remained in the room with me; it was pitch black, but I could hear breathing.

I stood still for what felt like the longest time, in fear of what was lurking in the dark. I knew someone or something was there. As the darkness faded, and my eyes adjusted, I tried to focus on the sudden movement in front of me. Before I could react, I was ambushed from all sides.

TWELVE

"SON OF A BITCH!" LEAHY CRIED THROUGH tears as he embraced me in a tight hug. "You're alive!"

"Sir, we thought you were dead!" Feinman yelled when the scant light adjusted in their eyes as well.

"Jeez, Feinman, you've all the cheeriness of a one-man funeral," I managed to retort.

I do not believe there were words to describe the emotions that came over me in that cellar when I realized my crew members were alive and not too worse for the wear. It was *Priority Gal's* full crew together again. They lined up to express genuine happiness to see me, all of our cheeks moist from tears. Of joy? I don't think so, but nevertheless they were good tears.

We sat for several hours in what appeared to be an old, dried-up wine cellar of some sort, glad to be together again and talking about all our experiences in the bailout. We jawed and relaxed just a bit, and I felt I was one of them, no rank. There was a true mutual respect, and we were all in the same boat together. Well, all except Feinman, who couldn't help but call me *sir*. I finally gave up, telling him to knock it off.

Leave it to Leahy to speak perfect German and schmooze the guard who brought us rusty water to drink and to talk. He shared with Leahy our fate. We would be put on a train in the morning and taken to a camp in Munich, the very place we had recently bombed the hell out of. The guard laughed, as if this were a game. I guess in many ways it was.

This holding cellar was relatively short lived, and less than a day later we were roused and told to line up and ready ourselves for a hike. I knew we were still in the Alps somewhere, and I prayed we weren't going to have to deal with mountainous terrain; my knee was just beginning to heal. This was the strangest feeling: every time doors opened while imprisoned, we never knew what was in the script for us. Would we be executed or allowed to live another miserable day behind locked doors?

My crew and I marched a few miles to an awaiting train depot. One by one we were identified by last name and shoved into the same cattle car. When it was Feinman's turn to get the shove, the guards stopped and prodded him with their rifles. The navigator stood and faced them, and a chill ran down my spine. Feinman was not responding, and that wasn't going to fly with the guards. The Nazis kept repeating the words "Feinman" and *"Jude."* I stepped from the rear of the line and interrupted the standoff.

"No, no—not Jewish Feinman. Irish Feinman. F-I-N-E-man. He's Irish." I hoped I sounded convincing. Feinman, on the other hand, looked guilty as sin and about to blurt something. I glared at him, trying to convey he would be forgiven at that moment for denying his religion. If not, we were all in jeopardy.

I knew Feinman understood my pleading gaze because he shirked off the confrontational look from his face and smiled, nodding, "Yes, Irish—I'm Irish." Feinman then gave the pantomime of drinking a mug of brew. The guards regarded him with smirks and encircled him and gave him a shove to get in the train car. At that moment I believed I was more relieved than Feinman.

By the time Leahy and I pulled up the rear of the line to be shoved into the cattle car, my leg had grown swollen and stiff from the walk. The platform was about chest high, and when it was my turn to step up, a soldier taunted me with his rifle, and I stumbled. Before I hit the wooden planks, Leahy grabbed me by the arm and yanked me upright, taking pressure off my right leg; then with amazing strength he hoisted me by the waist, up into the car.

When I rolled back to lend him a helping hand, I watched in horror as he took a gun butt from the guard, right straight to the temple. He faltered, and our eyes met briefly, his beseeching mine to assure him he wasn't just shot. I shook my head, still reaching for my friend. He somehow shook off what was sure to be a severe concussion and recovered his balance.

The guard screamed at him in German, and I knew Leahy understood clearly what the guy was saying. He reached for my hand and scrambled while I yanked him up into the cattle car. Just as his feet made it through the door, it was slammed and bolted, leaving all of us in the dark again.

I slumped onto the gritty floor of the train car and gently asked, "Men, you okay?" A few "yes, sirs," and then I heard sobbing to my right, and I knew without seeing through the darkness, it was Leahy. I reached for his shoulder and patted it because I didn't know what else to do. My own throat was thick with fear and sorrow for all of us.

Leahy vomited the entire way, and with the stress of travel—the train car being our toilet—one can imagine the stench when the doors were opened after a several-hour train ride. We had no indication where we were when the train stopped and we were unloaded. We did, however, know who was there, as the Gestapo greeted us on the platform with disingenuous smiles.

One at a time we received interrogation. We were slapped, punched, kicked, burned, and threatened with much worse. Because the Geneva Convention applied to Germany, they were careful not to harm us in ways that didn't seem plausible in a bailout situation. They continued to grill us on strategies, future plans, and number of aircraft they were dealing with. Occasionally they'd throw in a question that made little sense.

"Where were you born?"

"Who was your third grade teacher?"

"Does your family own a television, a car?"

I guess they hoped they could trick us into answering something. Still we didn't give up anything. Oddly enough, the Germans knew we were in the armada that bombed Munich a few days back, but they never asked about that day.

What both fascinated and terrified me about the Germans was their ability to get information—personal information—from other sources within hours of our capture. I knew the only thing that meant was that they had spies in the United States as well as in Britain. Nothing was off limits. Nothing was sacred anymore.

After leaving Gestapo headquarters we were herded back into another cattle car and transferred to Luftwaffe headquarters in Munich, where we received our first "meal." The sustenance consisted of bread made of sawdust, coffee from some kind of bean, and ersatz jelly. The entire time we were observed by only two guards. With nine of us and only two of them, one might question why we didn't try to overpower them and escape. The answer was simple. We were too busy waiting for them to suddenly, and without provocation, execute us. There was no room to even contemplate escape.

By the end of that day the officer POWs were separated from the enlisted POWs, who were herded back on the train for transport to a separate camp for men of similar rank. In turn, the four of us officers remained just a short walk from the train depot at a small encampment. We were locked up individually in solitary confinement. My cell was furnished with a cot, a straw mattress, and a glass bottle of murky water. There was a wooden crate in the corner, under which was a six-inch diameter hole in the concrete, meant to be my personal toilet.

On my second day I had a brief reprieve from solitary outside in a small, heavily guarded yard, and the air smelled putrid. I spotted two huge chimneys less than a mile away, and when the wind blew the smoke in the direction of our encampment, the stench was unbearable. With total lack of emotion, one guard explained in poor English that the smokestacks were in Dachau.

Dachau was already known as a notorious concentration camp. It made me wretch to learn that the Nazis used the prisoners there as slaves for their war machine, with thousands murdered or succumbing to disease, only to be burned in ovens or stacked like firewood. I asked myself what had become of this world. Then the more pressing question was addressed: Why were we being held in such close proximity to a Nazi death camp? There was certainly a method to their madness of bringing each of the prisoners outside. If this was a game, each time a prisoner learned the nature of the smokestacks, the Nazis earned points.

In solitary it became increasingly difficult to suppress my thoughts of family and home. For the first few days I used my memories as a means of survival, telling myself the story of my own childhood. I tried to recall the events that would make me feel good— walking to the bank for my mom every Saturday, getting slices of bologna from the butcher, the soda shop, and nickel movies. The smells were the things I missed the most: kielbasa and sauerkraut, pierogies, and kruschiki; the scent of soap and fresh sheets; holiday pine and cinnamon butter.

I entertained myself with memories of being a bingo runner for my dad. I was seven and cheating in the basement of the church. My father was the sheriff, and he was heralded as the luckiest player in town. Pop would then take the cheated winnings and anonymously disperse it to folks who needed it the most. My dad had decent values that were apparent to me from a very young age. Not only was he generous, he was kind. I remembered him bringing me along with him when he had to transport a prisoner across the lake to the jail. It was the most scared I ever was until bailout. He talked to the handcuffed man like a friend, which made a lasting impression on me. I guess it was all about respect.

I made a ritual of physical exercise and rationed my daily bread and dirty water as a distraction. I paced incessantly, figuring my leg was getting stronger, burning off some of my agitation. I knew what folks meant when they said they felt like climbing the walls. It was one step closer to insanity.

Sometime around my fifth day in solitary, I grew agitated. I had the sense I was losing my mind. I grabbed the hay mattress and flung it across my cell, knowing if I threw the cot along with it, I might draw the unwanted attention of the guards. I realized that if I still had some measure of self-control, then I still had my sanity. Relieved, I forced myself to pick up the strewn hay mattress and discovered something wonderful in the process.

Hidden within the thatched stalks of hay was a paperback book. I lifted *Goodbye, Mr. Chips* from the cement floor as if it were a delicate treasure. The pages were creased and parched yellow, but it was still in one piece. I had never read the book, and it was way off my typical genre of westerns and spy novels, but that made it even more of a treat. Over the next ten days, reading that simple British novel over and over saved my mind.

Henry Supchak photographed by the Germans following his capture. After confiscating his jacket, he was made to drag his parachute by tying it around his neck so that his hands could be visible at all times. (*Author*)

PART THREE

A World at War

THIRTEEN

WE SPENT ALMOST TWO WEEKS IN SOLITARY just outside Munich before the four of us were taken by train car to what would become our home for nearly half a year. During the six-hour ride, Feinman talked nervously and incessantly about how he would go to hell for the sin of denying his faith and was often told to shut up by Karlac. Karlac, in turn, was surly and bitter. I was sure his concerns went far beyond his dry cleaning at that point.

All the while, after that blow to the temple, Leahy never said a word. I noticed when we were released from solitary several hours prior, drool spilled from the side of his mouth most of the time. When I asked him a question, he either shook or nodded his head, but that was all. He had a faraway look in his eyes like he wasn't in there anymore. I was at a loss as to how to help him, which left me with a deep sense of guilt.

My leg was infected. I could tell by the smell it exuded when I moved. I had a genuine fear of losing a limb in war, after devouring westerns as a kid, and had gangrene dreams invading my childhood sleep every so often. I hoped at some point in the near future I'd have access to somewhat clean water, if for anything to clean my wound. The problem wasn't with the infection itself, but the pain it caused when I walked. I conceded it was another situation that would only get worse.

When we reached our final destination, Stalag Luft III, near the town of Sagan, about one hundred miles southeast of Berlin, we were referred to as "Kriegies," short for the German word "*Kriegsgefangener*," meaning war prisoner. From the get-go we were shoved into a large holding area. We were patted down for weapons and contraband. When it was my turn, I remembered the shrapnel Captain Metcalf had tucked in my flight suit the day I was shot down. Luckily it was missed, and I was ordered outside to line up at attention with the other prisoners.

For the next hour we stood rigid in the dirt, not having a clue what came next. I realized fear of the unknown was by far the worst sort of fear. The throbbing in my right knee was so unyielding, I prayed the movement wouldn't show through my pant leg. I had to remind myself frequently that I was an officer, and

I wouldn't give up. I held onto the fact that I was still alive, so someone or something from above must've been looking out for me.

We were barked at by a high-ranking Luftwaffe officer who facetiously shared the detailed story of the North Compound's most famous building, Barracks 104. "At one time, a year or so ago, North Compound housed the seventy-six British Kriegies— airmen just like you who thought they could cleverly escape the encampment by digging an underground tunnel." He paced back and forth, hands neatly clasped behind his back. "Took them the better part of a year to pull off their plan, but in the end all but three were recaptured and executed on the spot." He stopped to face his audience of POWs and beamed with pride like a schoolmaster. "And for the three escapees, won't they be constantly looking over their shoulder the rest of their miserable lives?" He chuckled.

After more threatening speeches by other German officials, we were systematically assigned to one of the five compounds. We walked like the living dead, each to our separate prison yards. Karlac and Feinman headed solemnly in the direction of the South Compound, and Leahy was in the Central Compound. When we parted, I realized I may never see any of them again.

"Hey, Wilson." I tried to get his attention by using his first name.

Leahy stopped and looked at me. He tried to smile, but his eyes showed such sorrow, and tears had left narrow tracks down his dirt-smudged cheeks.

"You take it easy now, pal, okay? I'll be asking about you, so stay out of trouble." I winked at him, but I knew he saw the sadness in my eyes as well. I watched my friend shuffle toward the gate of his compound and fade into the distance, and then I slowly made my way to the North Compound.

I was breaking apart inside. I wanted to scream, to run, to scale the fence. I was physically, emotionally, and spiritually close to bankruptcy, wrecked to the bone. The good news was that if I survived, I'd be released when the war was over. The bad news was that the most difficult part of this journey—the toughest role of my life, subhuman in some respects—had just begun.

FOURTEEN

THE SCUTTLEBUTT AND INSIDE REPORTS OF THE U.S. Army Air Force suggested that by mid-1944 at least 22,000 combat aircraft flew missions that targeted Nazi-held European facilities. Thus far, the cost to us had been a staggering 50 percent of those aircraft lost in aerial combat. More than 64,000 American air combat casualties had been tallied, and there was no end in sight. Approximately 39,000 men so far were missing in action—prisoners of war or internees or worse. I was now a number in these statistics.

During World War II, prisoner-of-war camps were situated worldwide for the purpose of confining enemy military combatants, as well as civilian personnel who were captured during wartime combat operations. Their imprisonment was to be terminated at the end of hostilities. The treatment of captives by their captors varied from one theater of combat to another. Generally, if the captor was a signed member of the Geneva Convention, the treatment of a captive could be classified as humanely reasonable and tolerable. If the captor was not a signer, brutal and inhumane treatment was the norm for their prisoners, and even outright murder.

The Geneva Convention defined an international agreement, signed in Geneva, Switzerland, in 1864. It established a code of operation for the care and treatment in wartime of the sick, the wounded, the dead, and of prisoners of war. It included the protection of all hospitals, medical units, and medical transport units displaying the emblem of the Red Cross.

In the Pacific theater the first line of defense was the sharks, since most of that war was fought over water. The lucky ones who survived ocean conditions were either thankfully rescued or taken prisoner of war by the Japanese. The Japanese did not recognize the Geneva Convention, and as a result inhumane and brutal mistreatment of captives frequently resulted in death or unconfirmed missing in action (MIA) reports. These Japanese camps could not be described as POW camps because of the brutality, torture, and starvation, and the hundreds of prisoners of war lost or unaccounted for. The term "death camp" better defined those prisons in the Pacific theater.

By comparison, the captives taken by the United States, Canada, and Britain were treated like tourists or vacationers. The "room and board" facilities enjoyed by them were probably better than that of a low-income American family at the time. Some American POWs returning home from years of torture and starvation took issue with the leniency with which the enemy was handled in the United States.

Germany was a member of the Geneva Convention and, for all intent and purpose, established POW compounds to confine all Allied troops and airmen captured during World War II. By and large, the German enemy provided the very bare necessities of food and shelter, and sparse medical care for the injured or sick captives. In general, it could be said that initially Germany did abide by the established code. Unfortunately, as the war intensified in its last year, the Germans became more ruthless and desperate. Life—or, more accurately, existence—in a POW camp could be described in a string of adjectives: boring, monotonous, frightful, shocking, grim, terrifying, restricted, depraved, deprived—the list could go on.

The population of Stalag Luft III POW compound was under the jurisdiction of the German air force, and held about ten thousand airmen. Most of the prisoners were American pilots, navigators, and bombardiers. The configuration of the compounds consisted of separate enclosures, divided by heavy-duty barbed-wire fences ten feet high. Ten feet within that fencing was another two-foot-high barricade of more tangles of barbed wire—this was the warning perimeter. If a prisoner went beyond the two-foot fence, they were assumed to be escaping and risked death. There were no gates connecting the camps. Each was identified in accordance with its relative location, such as north, center, south, east, and west camps. Nevertheless Yankee and British ingenuity prevailed, and surreptitious means of communicating with each other were soon found.

When I first arrived at the camp, the prisoners were allowed on occasion to use the open yard for exercise, and walking along the two-foot perimeter was a common form of outdoor activity. There was a road that ran outside the barbed-wire fencing—a dirt road used by Polish refugees to and from their field work. Once every few weeks, the refugees somehow figured out a way to find the one blind spot from the twenty-foot-high goon box. When the guard looked in the opposite direction, one of the refugees would take a few quick steps back and then lob a loaf of bread to the prisoners as though he were a quarter-back. The bread was then shared—maybe the equivalent of a half a slice each—among anyone walking along the perimeter that day who happened to notice. The ruse was all said and done rather quickly. The bread was never caught for fear a guard would happen to turn around, in which case it was swiftly stuffed under a shirt. Of course, all good things must come to an end. One unlucky prisoner got nabbed with the bread football, and the road was closed to refugees.

The North Compound was the first facility built to house downed airmen of the British Royal Air Force (RAF). They were among the first prisoners of war held by the German military. After America's entry into the war, the number of downed Allied flyers increased. To accommodate the influx, they increased from four to five camps, and British and Yankee prisoners were imprisoned together. I was assigned to the mostly-British North Compound.

The sole gate to the entire camp was located between the German commandant's headquarters and the North Compound. Next to the North Compound was the small medical dispensary for the entire camp. Needless to say, the North Compound had a lot of traffic, and it allowed me to get a sense of what was happening in the rest of the camp, including my crew. It was the compound where most escape attempts were made because of its proximity to the main gate. I had always considered myself a brave individual. When push came to shove, I tried to stand up for myself. In this place one thing was certain: I knew there was no way I was courageous enough to attempt an escape. The German guards had a talent for having you believe that they could read your mind. I tried to not even have eye contact with them if I could avoid it.

Within the North Compound was the highest-ranking British officer, a brigadier, which is a rank above a U.S. colonel. According to the brigadier—which is what we called him—he had been a prisoner for several years. Over the time of his captivity, he developed into an excellent camp commander who knew how to handle the German commandant.

The commandant of Stalag Luft III was a retired Luftwaffe pilot and World War I veteran. Because of his age, he was given the desk job of administrator of the prison camp. Brutality was the favorite tool of the German SS, but thankfully Stalag Luft III prisoners were encamped where a decent relationship existed between the brigadier and the Luftwaffe commander. For those in POW camps under poor command, it was a nightmare.

That is certainly not to say ours was a bed of roses. Prison was prison, and there was nothing positive about the conditions we were forced to withstand, not even for the higher ranked. We were being held against our will and convinced ourselves it could be much worse than body lice, dysentery, filth, starvation, and the occasional beating for good measure.

FIFTEEN

FINDING A POSITIVE AS A PRISONER OF WAR WAS like searching for a needle in a haystack of straight pins. Since our assignments to different compounds, I never saw Feinman or Karlac, but I received word on a regular basis that the two were alive and managing. I saw Leahy only one time in a full-yard roll call. His head lolled to one side, and his gait was still a shuffle. Worst of all, my friend and longtime comrade didn't recognize me. I felt my heart break of remorse that his injury and suffering were a direct result of his coming to my aid. Death was not the only result of war.

Every day, at least twice a day, all prisoners were ordered out to their respective yards to stand for long periods of time at attention. Often prisoners passed out from the tension, heat, or hypothermia and were left there on the ground. Whenever a prisoner disobeyed his captors, the Germans used the yard to set an example, as they would beat the man nearly to death. We were expected to remain at attention the entire time. On two occasions and without explanation, a prisoner was removed from the lineup and shot in the head.

Being one of the few American prisoners in the North Compound, I kept quiet, at least until I could translate some of the sharp but unfamiliar British jargon. The brigadier sought me out, sensing I was out of sorts. I could tell he respected me and he eased my anxiety by asking to hear about Vegas and American women. He was delightfully curious about the world and was interested in news he had missed since his imprisonment. I enjoyed exchanging stories with him, and he and I became fast friends.

The bond we shared put him in the fortunate position to assign one of the better guys in the Central Compound to keep a close eye on Leahy. The brigadier was able to get me bootleg antibiotics when my knee flared up. Some mornings my knee was so swollen with fluid I couldn't walk. On those occasions he covered for me with the guards, and I was permitted to stay in my bunk. The deal he struck with the guards was that the Yank—my nickname, short for Yankee—would do extra KP when I recovered. The deal he struck with me was that I read the Holy Bible the entire time I was laid up. He believed it was something one was obliged to do in situations such as these.

I had no choice but to take him up on the offer, and at first it was tough to focus, but low and behold, the next thing I realized I was reading the Bible when I wasn't laid up. I looked forward to getting back to it at the end of the day. A bit like Shakespeare, but so many more jaded characters, I thought. I knew neither God nor Jesus wrote the book, but whoever did deserved credit for the totally original piece of literature that it was. It took some time, but I read the entire thing, cover to cover. All we had was time, hence the expression "doing time."

The experience of prison camp made me think about time. From the beginning of time, life on this planet had always been a struggle for survival. The Bible writers didn't realize that in thousands of years, Geneva would have a convention. Had we learned anything at all from ancient history? A little, I figured, finding some comfort in not being the victim of a German crucifixion. Perhaps that was the needle of benevolence in the stack.

Starvation as a means to lose weight is not something I would advocate, but it certainly does the trick. Over the months I spent in Stalag Luft III, I went from the owner of a tall, decent physique to that of a boney teenager. The rations we received were mostly dried or rehydrated, with little sustenance or taste. Maybe once a month, each building received a couple of gallon containers of soup meant to feed more than one hundred men. Nevertheless, this was considered a real treat because it was a hot meal. The small German label on the cans claimed the contents to be some sort of "meat with fine noodles." We never questioned the ingredients and added equal amounts of water in an effort to make the soup last longer. The beautiful aroma of boiling soup filled the air on those fortunate days and drove the starving POWs to near frenzy. Hunger notwithstanding, each spoonful of soup and noodles was spiritually savored; we wanted it to last as long as possible.

The first time I was offered soup the wonderful taste nearly brought me to tears, as I could not recall the last time I had eaten anything hot and flavorful. Several of us newbies were seated among the experienced in the open area of the barracks, where the soup boiled on a makeshift stove. I quickly learned that special menus such as this were ceremonial in nature, and everyone gathered like it was a first Thanksgiving or a last supper.

While thoroughly enjoying my first soup in many months, a couple of newly imprisoned Brits— Cambridge University grads on the far side of the room—were having a hushed conversation over their soup tins, a behavior they would have been the first to point out was rude. The mumblings increased in volume, and word began to spread among the prisoners; all eyes focused on the soup. One of the Brits was studying entomology at university when the war broke out, and was educated sufficiently to identify the noodles we were enjoying as having not only two black specks on one end, but also leg-like appendages. Upon closer examination the entomologist proved correct in his classification: the hundreds of tiny white noodles were indeed maggotlike insect larvae.

"It's protein. Eat it, it's good for you," said the academic, and he continued to slurp what was left of his soup. After a slight hesitation on the rest of our parts, we followed suit and resumed eating. No one discarded their soup, and there were no leftovers. It went without saying that none of us would ever eat a bowl of soup in this lifetime without ascertaining whether the noodles had legs.

The low-ranking German guards, or "goons," as they were called behind their backs, held regular exercise every morning. We were allowed organized athletic activities and intercamp competition when approved by the commandant. The yards were heavily guarded and fiercely observed when prisoners were outside in numbers. Once in a while a prisoner would get too close to the fence along the compound perimeter, and some trigger-happy guard would take random shots, killing or injuring a prisoner in the process. Escape attempts were a common event in all camps, which kept the guards and special search units busy. Kriegie discipline and security were always in effect, especially after what was dubbed The Great Escape.

I learned from compound scuttlebutt about the specifics of that story. It was a simple matter of their daily exercise. The British prisoners took shifts during the night, digging a tunnel under some hidden floorboards within their barracks and coming outside every day with pockets of sand and dirt, which they drained down the inside of their pant legs, to mix with the rest of the grit in the yard. It was a slow, arduous, and tedious process. More than seventy prisoners escaped, but only three managed not to be recaptured. It proved, however, to be a major embarrassment for the Germans, as all the escapees were found outside the supposed foolproof perimeters of the encampment. The Germans executed most of those involved.

In lieu of escape attempts, some desperate prisoners went as far as breaking their own bones simply to get a somewhat clean bed for the night in the medical dispensary. After months or sometimes years without calcium, bones were brittle, making the task a little easier, but no less painful. Often that decision for many reasons proved to be a poor one—the main drawback being the dysentery that ran rampant through the camps. Parasitic ailments and contagions were responsible for the majority of deaths within the prison population. Over time, the medical dispensaries harbored a greater health threat than staying among the prisoners in the yards and barracks.

The Germans had taken away all our human rights and occasionally gave them back to us as privileges.

A good example was that once a month they allowed Red Cross packages, which contained essentials like socks, boots, and the occasional medical supplies. There were always a couple of personal parcels and letters, but not many. Cigarettes were used like money, making them a hot commodity. Bartering became common practice, as cigarettes were traded for anything from food to a poker payoff. There was little access to hot coffee, and milk was a luxury; alcohol was nonexistent.

In the months I spent in Stalag Luft III, I received one care package from my parents. It was postmarked four months earlier, but arrived a couple of weeks before Christmas. The opening of such parcels was done in the presence of guards, and the package was thoroughly ransacked for evidence of contraband or items they coveted for themselves. My package didn't seem of too much interest to the guards, as it contained homemade cookies that had grown rock hard over their four-month journey to reach me. There was a small sack of coffee beans, always a marvelous treat.

The last food item was a can of condensed milk, which felt like pay dirt. I held my breath as two of the guards tossed the can back and forth between them, pretending they came close to dropping it. Bored after a few tosses each, they put it back in the box. The pitifulness lay in the details: the very idea of hot coffee with cream made my mouth water in anticipation. The idea occurred to me that I would save it for

Christmas Eve and share my cherished gift with my four closest bunk mates.

The package also held a carton of cigarettes, which was immediately confiscated, and a *Life* magazine dated August 1944—with a full cover story about D-Day and President Roosevelt's reaction—also confiscated by the guards. I didn't care about the cigarettes. My pop knew I didn't smoke much, but that cigarettes had value in prison. It was the *Life* magazine I wanted. I was desperate for something to read. Having read *Goodbye Mr. Chips* dozens of times and completed the Holy Bible, I needed something a little more lively and current to sink my teeth into. I really had no choice but to surrender the items. After taunting me once more with the can of condensed milk, the guard tossed it back into the box. He shoved the box, which my father and mother had painstakingly packed, so hard across the table, it nearly fell to the floor. When I caught it midair, in a move of sheer desperation, the guards laughed and dismissed me.

The cookies were shared with some of the guys in my building—and stale or not—a mouse wouldn't have found a crumb.

December was a brutally cold time in Germany, with snow a daily occurrence. *Appel*, German for roll call, was held at least twice each day. Someone was always trying to escape, so after a failed attempt, roll call was more frequent, regardless of weather conditions or time of day. It wasn't unusual to find yourself in the yard at three in the morning, standing in six inches of snow in stocking feet. The guards, dressed in sheepskin and wool, took their time counting heads.

When Christmas Eve arrived, the idea of a hot cup of real coffee had several of my friends anxious with anticipation. Over the past two weeks, I found myself looking forward to having a hot cup of coffee made from real beans, with a splash of milk for sweet flavoring, as if it were a romantic date with Greta Garbo.

There were enough beans to share mugs of the hot tasty liquid with more prisoners than I thought. The condensed milk was another story, as I had squirreled that away, knowing there would only be enough for myself and my four other bunkmates to enjoy. Hot cups of coffee in hand, our only dilemma was opening the sealed can. After deliberating the options, I remembered the piece of shrapnel Metcalf had taken from my knee—a sharp piece of metal that had thus far eluded the guards during inspections. I kept it in a small crevice in the wood alongside my bunk. The saved shrapnel and a boot heel proved to be just the thing to puncture a small hole in the can.

Much to our disappointment, when the first drops fell into my coffee, I realized the milk must have spoiled because it was clear yellow and watery in consistency. We all gave a moan of disappointment, and worse for me, the turned milk had spoiled a great cup of coffee. Regardless, I toasted my parents for their valiant effort.

One of my bunkmates raised the can to his nose, and I waited for his grimace at the sour smell, but instead he slowly exclaimed, *"I'll be damned!"*

The can did not contain condensed or sour milk at all, but rather it contained whiskey. We were dumb-struck at first, but then behaved like schoolboys who had discovered a pinup magazine in the principal's desk. We kept it our little secret, and all of us savored every last drop. When the can was empty, I turned it over and discovered a tiny soldered hole in the center of the flat bottom. I knew my father, always full of ingenuity, figured out a way to replace the milk with whiskey. He must have spent hours perfecting his plan. He had patiently drained the milky contents through a pinhole and reversed the process and added the whiskey, probably with a syringe he procured from the local hospital. After all he was the sheriff, and that granted him access to a vast array of neces-sities. Last, he replugged the hole and added it to the parcel, unbeknownst to my mother, I'd bet. Pop knew she'd never object to adding the preserved milk for the coffee.

Each sip of the whiskey went down smooth and warmed our raw stomachs. It hadn't taken much for the four of us to feel flushed and a little giddy from the treat, and I relished the idea that it was the exact reaction Pop was counting on. The relaxation that overtook us, and the decent sleep we experienced for the first time in months, was so gratifying. I took personal pride in knowing that back in the little mining town of Nanticoke, Pennsylvania, my dad had figured out a way to outsmart the Nazis.

SIXTEEN

CHRISTMAS DAY CAME AND WENT IN NORTH Compound without as much as a blip on the radar screen. Temperatures into the New Year were below zero at times and finding warmth was nearly impossible. It was painfully obvious during each roll call that our numbers were thinning along with our bodies. A prisoner would go to dispensary, and the next day his bunk was replaced with a recently captured airman. Men were dying, and there didn't seem to be an end in sight.

The brigadier was a true leader when it came to keeping the morale of the men up. He sought out the commandant to get them extra privileges. He had bragged often to anyone who cared to listen about the seasonal plays held in South Compound. His fellow Brits loved theatrics, and he had permission to stage two plays a year, provided it didn't interfere with anything else. They were even given one of the warehouses in the South Compound to practice. It had a stage and a curtain and reminded me a little of the theater in *Our Gang*. The brigadier wanted me to be involved whenever he brought up the subject of the play, but I declined. I was not the dramatic type, and besides, so far there had been enough drama in my life.

Two weeks before Christmas, the brigadier had announced that this year's play would be one by Shakespeare. I smiled to myself, knowing he was mocking my interpretation of the Holy Bible as being a bit like Shakespeare; he was kidding. "The play will be *You Can't Take It with You*. As you all know, I will have been transferred out, so it's up to you to manage the theatrics without me. The director will be Jacque, and his assistant will be none other than my well-read Yank friend, Henry." Always one for a good joke, it turned out that this was the last assignment he gave me. The brigadier was soon to be moved to another prison camp.

Cheers went up around the room, and certainly not for me. Groups broke out all around me, as though that in and of itself had been well rehearsed. The men began discussing strategies and designs and costumes—everything they knew about the play. I heard the entomologist reciting lines and knew I was in for the long haul. I figured it was better for everyone involved if I stayed behind the scenes. I knew the brigadier had been directing these plays for a long while, and he knew I didn't know a single iota about the plot. I wasn't even sure plays had plots. It didn't seem to matter. An order from the highest-ranking Allied official within a fifty-mile radius left me no choice other than to accept my fate. The brigadier found the whole situation hilarious, and I found it terrifying. I couldn't insult him, so I went along.

By the second week in December 1944, the brigadier was transferred. He and I said goodbye, and he left me with a large supply of antibiotics. "Use 'em sparingly, mate." He gave me his address and told me to look him up if I were ever in Manchester.

"You can bet your arse I'll come to visit!" I told him in my worst Liverpool accent. I was sad when I embraced my new British friend for the last time, knowing we'd likely never see each other again.

After almost two months of rehearsals, the troupe was finally ready for their first performance. There were so many talented men, even men willing to portray women, just looking for a little positive diversion from the squalor around them, and the play provided just that. Myself, I was pleasantly surprised to find that the British prisoners were gifted, cooperative, and ingratiating when it came to this odd assignment.

The brigadier knew how to take a person out of his comfort zone and water him just enough for growth to occur. It soon dawned on me that he hadn't played a practical joke on me by giving me this assignment. He did it because he wanted me to get to know his people, so when he was gone, I'd have plenty of connections and friends. His method worked, and I garnered much enjoyment from being on set, as they say. It was probably one of the few times in prison camp that I laughed.

By the time we held the first performance, our old camp leader had been gone six weeks, and I missed the man immensely, but the show had to go on. On the eve of January 27, 1945, *You Can't Take It with You* was performed. It would become a night that the thousands of prisoners in Stalag Luft III would never forget.

SEVENTEEN

IN THE MIDDLE OF THE SECOND ACT OF THE PLAY, the reigning senior officer who replaced the brigadier walked onto the stage and announced in a tone suitable for eulogizing a stranger: "Hitler has given us thirty minutes to be walking out of here westbound. Let's move, men."

The scuttlebutt, and closer to the truth, was Hitler feared we'd be liberated by the Russian army closing in from the east across Poland, moving directly toward Sagan; they were only twenty-five miles away. Egomaniac that Hitler was, he figured that if he couldn't have the captives, no one could. It was in his best interest, and our own, that he hang onto us. He needed us as hostages, bargaining tools.

There was no way to understand Hitler's train of thought. On several recent occasions we were informed in no uncertain terms that we were very fortunate. Hitler had already arbitrarily ordered the murders of all the POWs. The guards hadn't followed through on those orders thus far because they, too— we hoped—realized their leader had lost his grip on reality, but who knew? We could easily be walking westward into a gas chamber.

After disappointed claps from the departing audience in the warehouse at the news we had received, I returned to my bunk and gathered my meager belongings: mostly saved food stuff, such as stale bread and some Red Cross biscuits known as hardtack. I stuffed the morsels in my coat pockets and was ready and waiting for the final evacuation order when I remembered my shrapnel. I secured my "can opener" in the hidden pocket of my woolen peacoat issued to us last month by the Red Cross, and moved with the crowd toward the exit gate of the compound.

The snow was knee-deep by the time we headed out. Ironically, those who hadn't heeded the advice of "don't take it with you" found themselves shedding belongings early on in our snowy southern journey. Other than minimal food rations and my shrapnel, all I carried was a small Oxford dictionary I had recently been given in trade for a handful of the antibiotics the brigadier had left to me. I felt so guilty taking anything in return for the much-needed medicine, but the Brit insisted I have the book. He said the brigadier told him to keep an eye on me. In addition to the shrapnel in my pocket, I held onto a few of the antibiotics, just in case my knee infection flared up. It was a few months since I had any issue with it, but the wound occasionally reopened and smelled bad.

It certainly had to be a sight to behold: ten thousand men trudging in a single line across a snow-laden terrain. Icy winds and inadequate winter clothing allowed the minus twenty degree temperature to shudder the body. Walking was extremely difficult and frozen feet were common, some even losing shoes without knowing because of numbed feet. The guards traveled this time without their dogs, which seemed unusual, but we figured the weather was just too cold for them and the guards cared more about their animals than the prisoners.

I thought about Leahy often during the trek and prayed he would survive this leg of our torturous journey. The guy was loving life and making jokes up until the split second before the gun met his temple. Somehow I knew he'd never be the same again.

If it weren't for World War II, I'd have never met Wilson Leahy, my trusted bombardier and close friend. Then that same war took him from me, stole him from everyone he knew and loved. When I thought of what happened to Lieutenant Leahy, and the rest of the atrocities of this war, I could clearly see the lines in the sand had been drawn for me. There came the before, the during—and hopefully—the after in my life. I was sure mental professionals would have a field day with the prisoners who survived.

Wilson Leahy, left, and Henry Supchak in Nebraska before deploying overseas. (*Author*)

The great exodus stretched for many miles along a ruddy southwestern route. A horse-drawn wagon followed the procession. Every now and again they would stop to pick up a collapsed frozen body. No one knew how many were picked up or how many were abandoned, silently buried under snowdrifts. British chaplain Murdo Ewen MacDonald would be able to tell how many. His assignment was to pick up the dead. He was a very busy man on that march, as the summons by way of whistle came for him again and again.

On January 29, two days after leaving Stalag Luft III, the German commander ordered a lengthy rest stop as the weary walkers stumbled into the town of

Muskau and found shelter wherever indoor space was available. For twenty-four hours, I slept in a slumped sitting position on the flooded floor of a tile factory with about three hundred other prisoners and a guard or two. The next morning before dawn the orders were given to resume the march toward Spremberg. The snow was light by this time; however, the ground had held at least two feet of fresh powder.

After a twenty-hour trek to the Spremberg rail station, we were jammed into boxcars typically used to transfer livestock. With fifty or sixty men in a car that could barely hold forty, the only way that we could sit was in a line toboggan style. Ventilation in the cars came by way of wide cracks between the side wall planks. We were locked in a moving cell for four days with only brief reprieves. The stifling, offensive smell of vomit and excrement defied description.

As the train neared Nuremberg it suddenly stopped, and we could hear the German air-raid horns sounding off. I immediately recognized the thunderous sound of a B-17 armada. The city of Nuremberg, with its airports and railroad yards, was an obvious target; and even if we couldn't see the bombs exploding as they hit the ground, we felt every impact. Some were distant, while others were close enough for debris to rain down on the cars. The train-load of thousands of POWs parked on the railroad siding were sitting ducks.

There were sighs of relief when the all-clear sirens sounded off and our train began to move. Our train and its track were apparently not damaged, but without windows in the boxcar I could only imagine the surrounding destruction caused by the bombs. I was grateful that the cracks in the planks weren't wide enough for a view because I had only previously observed bomb sites from several thousand feet above, never at eye level. A ground perspective was an unnerving one for a bomber pilot.

The next and final stop was Moosburg, a small town located just north of Munich and a short distance from prison camp Stalag VIIA. It was administered by the German army, and held officers and enlisted from all service branches and from several Allied countries. The boxcars were finally opened, and the prisoners began another march.

The weather cooperated, and the crisp fresh air was like being injected with a dose of life. Along the way, prisoners grabbed handfuls of snow and began to rehydrate themselves. I was filthy and disheveled and walked with a slight limp, but this time it wasn't because of my injured knee. I had frostbite on at least two of my toes. I soon learned I was one of the lucky ones. Many of the prisoners had frostbitten faces, fingers, chins, and even ears. A telltale sign was white on the tip of the nose or fingers or the rims of the ears, which sooner than later would turn black. Yet even those prisoners, who would inevitably lose chunks of their flesh, were grateful. They were not one of the many left for dead in the boxcars.

EIGHTEEN

S TALAG VIIA PRISONER-OF-WAR CAMP CONSISTED of numerous small compounds, separated by double barbed-wire fences, which enclosed dilapidated army barracks-type buildings. According to historians, the camp was built at the beginning of the war reportedly to hold a maximum of 14,000 inmates, and with our arrival, the population rose to more than 100,000 men of all nationalities and military ranks.

Although *Appel* was held twice daily to verify the head count, many prisoners were too weak to attend. With my damaged left knee and frostbitten feet, I struggled to stand some days. I waited a few weeks for my legs to mend and then set out on a regular basis to locate my enlisted men. Time after time it proved futile.

Sanitary conditions were abominable. The out-houses, with an open slit trench, were constantly in use. Dysentery was practically the norm at this point, and those afflicted stayed close to the "facility." Food was barely adequate at first, then as the population increased and supplies were not replenished, it became scarce. In February 1945 the Red Cross food supply had plain run out. Stale German "sawdust" bread and rotten potatoes were doled out in very small portions, as reflected in the bodies of starving prisoners.

The barracks were nothing more than empty shells on dank dirt floors. The improvised masonry wash-rooms had few cold-water faucets. Wooden bunks with straw mattresses were joined together into groups of twelve, in order to cram five hundred men into a building designed to house a maximum of two hundred occupants. Little light from outside or inside could get by the stacks of bunks. Single lightbulbs strung far apart and high above the center aisle pro-vided weak illumination, but that seemed to matter little because it helped conceal the bedbugs, lice, fleas, mice, and rats that shared our bunks.

Over a short period of time it became evident that many of the men, although they showed no external wounds, had lost a bit of their minds. Like Leahy, they walked the yards in a haze—confused, talking to themselves, and often crying. I didn't know when that happened to a man, but I knew the breaking point was always looming close by. There was the occasional suicide, and that was a tough decision for me to reconcile because I believed each one of us had been born with a survival instinct. In prison camp it was all about getting to the next day, and suicide didn't make sense to me until I heard about tail gunner George Halpern.

Sergeant Halpern was in a B-17 that was shot up so fatally that bailout was ordered. Unfortunately, just after Halpern jumped and pulled the rip cord, nothing happened. His chute had malfunctioned, and Halpern continued to free-fall, picking up speed with nothing to slow him down but the ground. In a state of panic—knowing he was a goner—Halpern thought he was having a heart attack and evidently passed out less than a hundred feet up.

When Halpern came to, he was imbedded in a massive mound of freshly thatched hay. His body had gone completely through to the ground, but the hay was obviously enough to slow him down. Although he was rendered with a sprained back, he was able to walk away. No one would have believed the story except that four other men from the crew, who had witnessed their tail gunner's fall from the sky without a chute, landed in the same pasture as Halpern miraculously climbed from the hay, after which they were all rounded up for prison camp.

Fellow prisoners of war referred to Halpern as a magician, a god, a lucky bastard, but the truth of the matter was that Sergeant Halpern was never the same again. Falling more than ten thousand feet without a

American airmen in one of the compounds at Stalag VIIA in April 1945. (*USAF*)

parachute had to be one of the most terrifying experiences fathomable. It may have only lasted two or three minutes, but imagine what runs through a man's mind when he realizes he has no chute.

Halpern walked around the prison yard stiff as a board from the back injury and never said a word, and when he did, his mumbling rivaled that of Leahy's speech. He swatted at things that didn't seem to be there, and every so often he would have an outburst, but at no one or nothing in particular. The POWs ignored him, but I felt so sorry for the man. I wondered if and when this god-awful war ended, would Halpern insist on taking a ship back to the United States? I later learned Halpern wouldn't be going home after all. He had hung himself from a rafter in one of the barracks.

As the spring weather began, some of the more enterprising prisoners moved out of their infested bunks and into makeshift "tents" that had been erected to house the stream of newcomers arriving daily. Some chose to sleep on the ground, and it resembled a giant hobo village. At night, I found some solace in being outdoors, where the garbage couldn't be seen and the stars somehow gave me hope.

I found I required only a couple hours' sleep. I figured I must be draining whatever adrenaline I had in storage because as malnourished as I was, I had energy to keep going long into the night. It was at night that I could search for my men with ease. I eventually found all the enlisted crew members. The camp was vast, and I went through at least twelve compounds before I found my men. They were pretty torn up but had stuck together. The conditions they had endured before coming to Stalag VIIA did not involve plays and soup; rather, it was just a step up from the concentration camps. It would be a long while for these men to regain the weight they had lost and to get over whatever diseases they may have contracted.

Rocco, the ball turret gunner, who froze in the hatch during bailout, had stepped up as a leader with the men in prison, according to Thomas. Thomas was trying his best to hold it together, but that was all he was capable of doing. The guys responded to Rocco, and I made sure he knew how proud I was of him. The bravado I once knew Rocco to possess was gone, replaced by what could only be identified as humility and gratitude.

I tried to spend time with the guys as often as I could without jeopardizing my standing with the guards. With a camp this large, the German guards grew more and more paranoid by the week. I told the men to stay put and not to try and find me. I'd come to them. Many a night Rocco and I sat and talked about East Coast living, New York, and our favorite foods.

"Hey, sir," I remember him claiming one night, "where I come from the restaurants are better than the neighborhoods." Rocco grew up in a tough section of Brooklyn. Then he confidently said, "When we get home, you come visit me. My mamma will make you the greatest Italian feast you ever saw."

All the men talked of getting together when we got out of this war zone. Crazy, outlandish plans were made, and I was sure they would never happen, but that didn't matter. I found such warmth and camaraderie in getting to know my enlisted crew better. These were great men, and in spite of the prison conditions, we still managed to have a few laughs.

I tried to keep the men updated on Leahy as often as I could. They didn't know Feinman, and Karlac wasn't their favorite, although they always asked about him. Leahy was the one we were genuinely upset over. Rocco always promised that he would keep me posted if there were any issues with the five of them.

Feinman was hanging in there. It was rare when I saw him, because he said his goal was to stay as inconspicuous as possible, fly under the radar, he had said. I knew he still carried a grudge for me for encouraging him into denying his heritage when he had a gun aimed at the back of his head, but this war was not about his religion, or him. It was a war of senseless killing by a maniac and his sadistic, brainwashed followers. What good would it have done him to claim his belief system to a culture that hated Jews? Feinman never minced words with me, but told me that in his efforts to lay low in this hellhole prison camp, I was not helping by coming around and checking up on him all the time.

Notwithstanding the Germans, Karlac was his own worst enemy. He almost gave me the impression he held me responsible for *Priority Gal*'s demise. Although he never said it, I was the one who was supposed to get them home safe, and I didn't do that. I knew that if he was placing blame for this on me, and not seeing war for what it really was, it would be quite problematic for him down the road. Regardless, I sought him out on a regular basis to see how he was getting on.

Leahy wasn't doing well at all and barely said a word when I occasionally was fortunate enough to track him down. He had blackened toes and was sick much of the time from the dysentery. I recall the last time I found him he was behind a pile of trash, lying in a fetal position. He sat up when he saw it was me. I talked and he listened. I encouraged him that the war would be over soon, that it had to be, and he would be home with Jodi before he knew it. I made sure he was fed, and I gave him the rest of my antibiotics. The last thing I recall him saying to me in his garbled speech was, "Henry, I'm losing this war."

NINETEEN

On April 29, 1945, it wasn't the usual morning sounds that startled me awake. Over the past few months, the prisoners had grown accustomed to the milling around and chatter of guards, trucks rolling on gravel both hither and yon, barrack doors banging open for wake-up calls, and roll calls and toilet calls. On this particular morning those sounds were drowned out by the sound of heavy gunfire, explosions, and the distinctive rumbling of tanks. The war had come to Moosburg and Stalag VIIA.

The prisoners were unarmed, of course, so we had no choice but to keep out of the way and pray things would go in our favor. The guards assembled to defend the camp.

Just over the horizon of what appeared to be a vast wasteland came a column of tanks and jeeps. Dust billowed around them, and they almost seemed a mirage all in sepia tones, only this was real because we didn't just see it—we heard it and felt it. One of the prisoners, an Australian, found binoculars and announced to the hordes of men in the yard that it was the United States Army, the good mates. We all let out gasps of relief and screams of exhilaration.

Without stopping, a jeep came crashing through the barbed-wire fencing, ripping through it as though it were spiderwebbing, and collapsing it. It was followed by more jeeps and finally a tank. The German guards were forced almost immediately to throw down their arms and surrender to the superior American force. Suddenly and from everywhere, prisoners sprang from the precarious safety of their hiding places and raced forward to greet and, in many cases, embrace their liberators.

"Does this mean the war is over?" We were shouting questions and making assumptions to no one in particular. "Let the Nazi sons' of bitches rot in hell!"

"Congratulations, men, you've won the war! You're free!" The American officer in charge of the task force announced.

Small riots broke out, not necessarily violent, just a long-awaited expression of "I can, so I will." Of course, none of us were too confident of anything. It was all speculation giving us such a high. The idea of the war being over was almost too much to bear.

When the dust settled, what was left behind were thousands of ex-POWs, two jeeps full of supplies, and several American soldiers assigned to oversee the dis-encampment process, whatever the hell that meant. After all the clothing was passed out to those who needed it most, and the medications were handled in a similar fashion, it was time to relax and digest the food we were given: fresh bread, steamed rice, bananas, and hot tea. It wasn't much, but it didn't matter—it was the best meal I had ever eaten. Besides, it didn't take the surgeon general to figure out that POWs initially shouldn't eat anything other than what they're used to: bland was best. Foods, especially rich foods, needed to be reintroduced slowly.

We were all a little in shock. The war ended just like that. It was over, and it felt as though we were the last to find out. Yesterday it had been business as usual in the camps, the guards carrying on as prison employees do; then after a show of force, they had surrendered, giving us no time to process the situation. Thoughts raced through my mind with the abrupt sensation of freedom: wait until my parents got word that I was still alive. The image of their reactions gave me gooseflesh. I was so happy for them and wished I could be the one to deliver the news.

Funny thing how prisoners never talked about this part of the freedom rollout. Odd how one leaves out these best parts: the family learning the truth, the delicious appreciation for your first real food, initial freedom from the adrenaline that was a constant companion. Instead, we all talked about what we would do when the war was over. We might marry a girlfriend, eat an entire pizza, or buy a car—but we never discussed these things. The war had ended, and these mundane thoughts were not even close to what I had imagined I'd think when the moment came.

After dispersing all the food parcels and other necessities, a trumpeter from one of the jeeps stood and began playing the U.S. national anthem. The prisoners froze in their steps and rose from their seats—hats off, right hands to hearts. Two army guards ceremoniously removed an American flag from a satchel, carried it over to the flagpole, where in one fell swoop the waving swastika was lowered, released from the halyard, and the American flag was raised to the top. There were no words to describe that particular experience. As our flag billowed and cupped in the Bavarian spring breezes, color seemed to come back into the world. It unwittingly brought most of us to our knees.

TWENTY

On May 1, 1945, General George S. Patton arrived by jeep to formally liberate the men of the notorious Stalag VIIA. Patton gave his word that within twenty-four hours, reinforcements would arrive with more food and, more important, transportation out of this godforsaken death pit.

It had been said Patton had a real way with words, and now I had the priviledge of witnessing his eloquence up close and in person. His visit was brief, yet he managed to mingle with thousands of prisoners who greeted him as a conquering hero. He seemed to revel in the attention as much as his audience celebrated their freedom. Before General Patton saluted his farewell, he gave parting remarks.

"Thanks, men, for a job well done. Look me up for a drink when you're back in the states." The freed

POWs broke up in laughter. "Now, if you will excuse me, I have work to do and a war to wrap up." The applause was deafening and seemed to go on for hours, and shortly after the laughter subsided we were loaded onto trucks and officially freed from Stalag VIIA.

I was transported with thousands of POWs, and I hadn't run into my men since we were freed. It was not for lack of trying. The evacuation to medical camps had to be done in shifts, and the endeavor was carried out quite efficiently. My group of several hundred American officers, after a two-hour truck ride to Regensburg, was left in a huge hangar that was used by the Luftwaffe for their fighter planes situated not far from Munich. The hangar had a couple of discarded Messerschmitts in complete disrepair off to the far side, and during our ten-hour stay a few of us decided to explore. We all wanted some sort of souvenir. Sure, I had my shrapnel, but that didn't count. In the cockpit of one of the fighters, I happened upon a red armband with the black Nazi swastika emblem. It served my purpose—evidence that I had been here, and I shoved it in my pocket.

The exodus toward a nearby airport was surprisingly well directed and disciplined, despite the poor physical condition of many POWs. There was no pressure, no rushing or running. It was an orderly slow walk to the airport—a real freedom walk. The general attitude among the evacuees was logical: Why hurry when we had waited all those months and years to be freed? And, quite frankly, what plans could we possibly be rushing off to after being gone for so long? Other than being reunited with my family and friends, I had no agenda.

Shortly after arriving at the airfield, an armada of Douglas C-47 transport aircraft arrived. Again, in orderly fashion, each plane was loaded with American former POWs, all comfortably seated and served a nonalcoholic beverage of their choice. Without a doubt, thoughts of the conditions of traveling in the boxcars crossed everyone's mind—it most certainly did mine. The flight from Moosburg, Germany, to Liège, Belgium, took about three hours. The sky was clear, and we flew smoothly at a relatively low altitude. We were able to view the beautiful passing scenery enroute.

Upon landing at Le Havre, our final stop, we were transported in comfortable buses to Camp Lucky Strike, about eight miles away. There were only a few permanent hospital structures in the American compound. The rest were huge tents, quite comfortable on the interior, which served as special activities centers. No one was permitted to enter the grounds without first passing through the delousing facility. After discarding our clothing in a private cubicle, we were treated with a harsh, odiferous chemical used to kill the most resistent pests. It burned the skin and eyes, but no one ever complained; in fact, some went through a second time before they were confident their body was pest free.

The privacy of another tent housed shower stalls and hot showers with plenty of lathery soap. There was no time limit at this stage, because we were each hard pressed to recall the last time we had a real shower. An hour for this particular shower felt about standard.

Next on the schedule was oral hygiene, with dentists and hygienists on hand to assist. There were some with very serious dental problems. Others would never be able to show off their pearly whites again.

Everyone was issued a pair of khaki trousers, shirt, underwear, socks, shower sandals, and a baseball-type cap. Clean clothes were another treat. Sliding on the soft cotton undergarments, then the crisp pressed slacks, was a surreal sensation. The shirt and socks were even better. I guess the extreme degree to which I appreciated cleanliness at that point was in direct proportion to the depth to which I had lost it.

Then came the dream tent. After starving for months, dozens of tables in the center of the tent were loaded with hot food, fresh breads, eating utensils, and napkins. Selecting the hot food was no problem. By order of the Medical Department only one type of hot meal was available: Chicken à la King and hot biscuits. A sign above the table cautioned the men to "eat very slowly." Come back to second or third helpings—but—*eat very slowly*. A food technician at the exit end of the food line briefly explained that one must give the digestive system an opportunity to absorb food intake. If rushed or stuffed, stomachaches would inevitably result.

And it did. Understandably, after starving for a long period, the tendency to devour food was hard to control. I was cautious and still got sick after a few spoonfuls. I gave up for a while, but after cleaning up and taking a brief nap I was back in the chow line for more of the same. The second time around I fared a lot better. The food line, along with the shower stalls, stayed open twenty-four hours a day, allowing for the men to slowly reacquaint themselves to their life before prison camp.

After a day or two of relaxation, scheduled medical checkups began. A team of doctors and nurses were on hand to make sure everyone was examined. The infirm had already been handled prior to our arrival at Camp Lucky Strike, but now some of the less injured were hospitalized for treatment. Everyone seemed comfortable, preoccupied with thoughts of home and family, but mostly relieved we had survived.

Our stay in Camp Lucky Strike lasted about ten days. We were issued crisp new uniforms of our respective military organization, and preparations for departure began. The seven-day Atlantic voyage back home aboard a transport was just over the horizon. There was no fanfare or parties to mark our exit from Camp Lucky Strike. The only real thing we took with us was the true meaning of freedom and the memory of the thousands of young men who lost their lives in order to guarantee it.

PART FOUR

Home

TWENTY-ONE

MY HOMECOMING WAS LESS THAN SPECTACULAR. Sure, when I stepped from the bus that delivered me from the docks of New York and onto a bus for a three-hour drive to Atlantic City, New Jersey, it seemed enchanting. Atlantic City was headquarters for repatriation of returning POWs. There we were relicensed, refingerprinted, and issued new social security cards. At times I almost felt like a prisoner again. Within three days I was back home in Nanticoke, Pennsylvania, for a three-month leave.

Upon seeing me at the bus station, my mother and sister broke down in tears. My dad and I embraced. He then held me at arms' length to have a better look at me.

"Hey Pop, I owe you a drink, don't I? Or is it a glass of milk?" I winked at him.

He pulled me into his warm embrace again. "Ah, the condensed milk caper was a success, huh?" He laughed, and I guess the release of one emotion led way to another because he turned from me and wept. I knew he didn't want attention drawn, so I made my way to my sister and mother and let them dote all over me.

Initially, I felt every day at home was like a birthday. I went to sleep under clean sheets, a cool pitcher of water by my bed, and woke up to sounds of birds singing and sunshine. I could come and go as I pleased. The scents of a hot meal were always floating through the house from Mom's kitchen, and I began to put some weight back on. I reconnected with friends I didn't even know I had and was lauded in town, thanks to a campaign by my proud dad.

Soon enough, as predicted, life became business as usual. I grew antsy and bored. I began having nightmares, on occasion being suddenly awakened by screams that turned out to be my own. I could tell over a few weeks' time, it was taking a real toll on my family. There was no possible way for them to understand, and no way for me to explain, what I had gone through without upsetting the applecart even more. I needed to be among the people who truly understood where I had been when I was in Germany. I loved my family dearly, but it was as if in just a few years away, I had completely outgrown them. When my three-month leave from the air force was up, I didn't waste any time packing my belongings and heading out to my new assignment in San Bernardino, California.

At the time I was convinced California had more to offer than any other place in the world, from geography and climate standpoints. Before long, I found myself falling back into a rhythm and enjoying my new freedom. I tried not to think about the combat missions, the prison camp, and the crew I no longer knew. That proved to be a tall task, and those memories found their way into my dreams every night.

Henry Supchak, right, alongside his commanding officer at San Bernardino, California, in 1946. (*Author*)

By day, I walked around dressed in a uniform sporting all sorts of ribbons from a Purple Heart to the Distinguished Flying Cross. Early on in the Golden State, I drew the attention of a studio producer who asked me questions about my war experiences, and then invited me to a film set he was working on. The studio was looking for a technical advisor on a war movie planned for theaters in 1948. The name of the film was *Twelve O'Clock High*, and the actor in need of technical advisement was Gregory Peck.

My only experience with sound and stage was in prison camp, but the execs didn't care. They wanted me for my pilot expertise. With the go-ahead from the air force, I spent the next two weeks working side by side with Mr. Peck for an hour or so each day.

The first time I watched him in the cockpit of the bomber facsimile, I had to comment. He was holding and turning the steering column with one hand, as if it were a car on a stretch of highway. "With all due respect, Mr. Peck, a B-17 is a heavy bomber, and it takes some muscle to fly it." I was in uniform and hoped he didn't ask studio security to show me out.

"Major, is it?" He didn't wait for an answer. "I want to thank you for your service during the war. It's an honor to have you on my set."

After that he and I got along just fine. I knew that when they closed that stage set, I'd not be buddies with the man, but I was grateful for the experience. I looked forward to the premiere, but in all honesty, not as much as I had looked forward to *You Can't Take It with You* in Germany just a year earlier.

A couple of years in California and I was exhausted. My personal life was a disaster. I decided to accept an assignment in Alaska, a region of the world I had always been fascinated with. My family and friends disapproved, saying it would not be a good idea to be so far away. Some even accused me of running away and not having my priorities straight.

The decision to move, lock, stock, and barrel, to Fairbanks, Alaska, proved to be one of the best decisions I'd ever made. It was one of the most memorable times of my life. The animals, the stars, the scenery, and the people added to my positive learning adventure. The experience was a much-needed reprieve from external controls over my life. Unfortunately, I still took with me the internal, but I came to believe in the value of my time there. I wasn't as much running away from something, but rather running toward being on my own, free. It always boiled down to staying free.

The military was lax with its Alaskan bases, perhaps figuring it was just too darn cold and dark for the troops to do anything crazy. Left to our own devices up there, we did our job and spent the remainder of the time discovering a culture few Americans understood, like nose kissing and igloos with fireplaces. Days that lasted twenty-three hours, or nights that lasted as long, creatures that looked prehistoric, and glaciers—pristine glaciers—shifting the earth beneath.

Our jobs took us through man-made tunnels leading to undercover stations, the likes of which I had never seen before. There were other assignments sending us into the wilderness for weeks at a time. When I was completely out of communication in a

location where no one on the planet could find me—
that's when I felt the most secure. I was able to think
about things and sort them out at my leisure. I often
thought of my crew and hoped they were faring as well
as me. I had ways of contacting them, but I wasn't
quite ready for that yet. I needed to put some distance
between myself and the war.

Back on base, after a rather lengthy trip to a radar
station in the far north, I returned to my room to find
mail, a rarity. One letter had my mom's handwriting,
and my heart sank. I prayed it wasn't bad news. I
knew no matter where we were stationed, the military had an obligation to deliver news of family emer-
gencies directly to us. I didn't think it would come by
regular mail.

When I opened the envelope, I found a note from
my mother, scratched on her best stationary. She sent
her love, said all was well at home, and made refer-
ence to another envelope within, received at our
Nanticoke address. The envelope displayed a stamp
of an American flag and a postage mark from
California. Curious, I tore open the envelope and
read.

August 1952

My dearest Henry,

It is with great sorrow that I must inform
you Wilson passed away on July 12 of this
year, just shy of his 30th birthday. I tried

finding you in San Bernardino, but they said you had been transferred and they wouldn't tell me where. Knowing you, you're probably on some secret mission.

Anyway, I want you to know, my beloved husband, Lieutenant Wilson Leahy, thought very highly of you. He was never well after the war as you know. Before the brain tumor ravaged his thoughts, he said your name often and always with what I perceived as his old true smile.

Henry, I hope this finds you well and healthy in mind and body. You take care of yourself and be well.

Warmest regards,

Jodi Leahy

For the first time since my seeing the American flag raised when I was freed, I cried. This time it was out of sheer grief. I was mad at myself for never visiting him when we got back. We both lived in California, and I convinced myself I wanted to remember my friend the way he was before the gun butt to the skull, but I knew that was crap. I was afraid I wouldn't know what to say to Leahy. I didn't think I would have the words. For the first time in my life I felt like a real coward.

Priority Gal had lost her first crew member, and although it had been eight years since she crashed, it still felt like yesterday. I made a vow I would get back on the horse and locate the rest of the crew. Of course, I knew my nightmares would flare up and I'd be forced to battle my demons once again, but I needed to move back to civilization, both physically and mentally.

Shortly after the letter from Jodi Leahy, I decided I'd spent enough time in subzero temperatures, and it was time for a change in scenery. When my assignment was up in Alaska, I opted for the other huge state offering warmer climes—Texas. When I first heard the name of the town over the radio, the commander said "Amarillo," and I heard "armadillo." My reaction was "Count me in!"

In looking back on the five years I'd spent on the tundra, I took close to a thousand slides: pictures of snowflakes and bison, cars driving on lakes, and native Eskimos interacting in subzero temperatures. So many photos from Alaska, and yet I have not one single picture of myself posing with Gregory Peck. I assumed, or at least prayed, that meant perhaps I had some of my priorities straight after all.

TWENTY-TWO

THE KOREAN WAR WAS COMING TO A CLOSE, AND the military was changing before my eyes. Bases across the country now accommodated troops of women. Flight nurses and service girls of all shapes and sizes changed the very foundation of the air force that I was introduced to ten years earlier. Amarillo Air Force Base was no exception.

Although my rank was that of major, my war experience allowed me decent assignments. I was managing the air base's food services. It involved a canteen for meals and an officer's club. There was a huge population of enlisted men in Amarillo, and they ran their own bar and set of mess halls.

I had never done much food preparation. It didn't take long for me to discover I had a passion for it. Preparing wholesome and nutritious meals and then presenting them in a way that appealed to the five senses became an interesting and fun challenge. Every day from 1100 to 1300 hours the officer's mess served a cafeteria-style lunch. It was our busiest time of the day, and the chefs and staff worked in complete synchronization. I positioned myself in different places throughout the lunch hour to monitor the way my staff got the job done.

I had been in charge of food services for about a year and was observing the line of officers placing food orders when I noticed a female officer—a beautiful flight nurse—having a grand old time laughing with her friends. Her laugh was infectious and she had my attention, so I did what I was already doing: I observed.

According to the bars on her uniform, she was a lieutenant, and she moved through the line like a pro. I had not noticed her before and was surprised at the amount of food she piled on her tray: two desserts alongside a sandwich; a soup and a salad; plus bread, butter, and a fruit cup.

I glanced around the room, wondering where she was going to sit; and when I looked back, I saw her approach the register, adjust the cashier's tie and peck him on the cheek. She then moved from the line with a smile on her face that could light the room. The sole issue I had with the whole scene was not that her public display of affection was not becoming of an officer, especially with an enlisted man, or that her food consumption bordered on gluttony—it was that she didn't pay.

Not that I wanted to be a jerk, but she had just stolen food with the help of the cashier. Being that the previous day was payday, why couldn't this officer pay for her food? I decided to give this woman and my cashier the benefit of the doubt, so I waited until the next time the air force nurse showed up again for her free meal.

Lucky for me it was the very next day. Once again I watched as she loaded her tray with more food than the previous day. The cashier was of course the same sergeant, and I decided to approach him first. When I asked him whether he gave her the food for free, he looked like he might have a stroke. I threatened everything from Leavenworth to court-martial, and eventually the real thief came over.

"I couldn't help but notice that you're yelling at this kind sergeant and pointing in my direction." She was even more gorgeous close up. "What gives with making a scene, Maj?"

Maj? Who did she think she was talking to? Okay, so I was a major, but Maj? "Did you pay for your food? Lieutenant, is it?" I squinted as if I couldn't see any medals. She appeared to be a well-decorated Korean War MASH (Mobile Army Surgical Hospital) nurse.

"Oh, you have to be joking. So what? He let me slide this one time on a dessert or two. Don't take it out on him. I said I'd pay him back next week. Right, Chuck?"

"His name's Pete. Chuck's the evening cashier you obviously have snowed as well." I took her by the arm and gently ushered her away. "Lieutenant, you're lucky I don't have him court-martialed for theft."

She laughed. "Court-martialed? For lettuce and rice pudding?"

"You have enough on that tray to feed a small country."

"So, Maj. Are you saying I'm a thief and a pig?" Another fit of laughter.

"So why is it you have no money less than twenty-four hours after payday?"

She stopped laughing at that. "That's really none of your business." She looked down and then back up at me. "If you must know, I owe Colbert's my paychecks for the next few weeks."

"Colbert's. Isn't that the department store downtown?" I couldn't understand how someone could owe a clothing store.

"Yes, that's the one." She sighed. "They let me run a tab because the owner knows my father, that he doesn't have a job, so I send my parents money every month. I wouldn't do it except I have a little sister still in high school who lives with them. That's why I joined the air force. It meant a steady paycheck, so I could take care of Nancy—that's my sister, you'd love her. She's great!" Her face lit up when she spoke of her little sister. I realized this lieutenant was one special person, and after that first conversation, I had to get to know her better.

Turned out she was good for me—loosened me up a bit—and maybe lowered my walls a few feet. I liked being around her because she was a ray of sunshine, the likes of which I had never met. She continued to refer to me as "Maj," even though I asked her not to, especially in front of the base commander. Turned out, the man adored her and she could do no wrong. She reminded him of his own daughter, he told me when he heard we were dating. His advice to me was relax and go with it. Lieutenant Elizabeth was one beautiful dish.

One night she seduced me into reopening the officer's club after hours. At one point that night I recall her wearing my epaulet leafs to hike her skirt up over her knee in a show of sexy bravado. This woman, who was more than ten years younger than me, was on the bar dancing. I wondered how things had gotten so out of control and realized that I had fallen for her. Love sure was complicated.

We were together for the better part of the next year, whenever we had liberty from our responsibilities. Over that time I had received a promotion to lieutenant colonel, a rank I never thought I'd see, and all in all I was grateful to the military for giving me this recognition. It always paled, however, against the nightmares that I was still having.

When I nearly killed Elizabeth one night while I was still asleep, I had to confide in her about my demons and regrets. After telling her about Leahy, she became persistent about my contacting the rest of my crew members. I was scared to admit I had weak-nesses, but she knew. Elizabeth had several of her own demons from her year as a MASH nurse. She believed I was a hero, and I could finally put it in the past if I talked about it and reunited with the rest of the crew.

Okay, so Leahy was gone, and he was already too far gone even when he was alive, but there were eight other guys, ten if I counted Krusan and Hettler. It would take time, but she promised to help me through all of it. The more she pushed, the more I backed off, until push came to shove and I ran.

I was given an opportunity for early retirement from the air force, and I jumped at the chance. When I told Elizabeth, she said she wasn't surprised and she wished me the best. We spent the night together before I left for my hometown to regroup. She said she too had two more months left and had decided not to stay in, that she'd be returning to her home in Brooklyn, where her sister was in college.

Although we parted that next morning, I never stopped thinking about Elizabeth, but I knew it was best to stay away and let her live her life without my baggage. Still, not a day went by that I didn't wonder what she was doing and how she was doing it. About two and a half months after I arrived home to Nanticoke, I received a letter postmarked from New

York City. I knew without opening the lavender-scented envelope that it was from Elizabeth.

Debating whether I'd be opening a can of worms by opening the letter, in the end curiosity and hope got the best of me, and I tore into it. There was a small note card inside with an invitation to Saint Patrick's Cathedral in Manhattan for the following week.

I miss you and I'd love to see you.
Meet me and I'll know you feel the same.
E xo

TWENTY-THREE

IT WAS A PERFECT SUMMER DAY IN THE CITY. THE sun was high overhead when I exited the cab on East 54th Street, outside the historical, ornate church.

Elizabeth was kneeling in the last pew, head down in hands. I stood silent for a moment, recalling how serious her faith was to her, having been practically raised by nuns. I took in her honey-hued waves, the small hat pinned in place, her slim neck and wrists. She looked like an angel.

As if sensing I was behind her, she turned, and when she saw I was standing there, a bouquet of flowers at my side, she ran to me and we hugged. Eons seemed to pass in silence while we stood rocking and embracing each other. When we finally separated and looked into each other's eyes, I saw she had been crying.

It was time for me to get up my nerve, and before I knew it I was down on bended knee before her, flowers in hand, proposing marriage. I barely got the words out. "*Yes, yes,*" she exclaimed, leaving me with no doubt as to whether I was doing the right thing.

After a romantic lunch in Greenwich Village, we made our way back to the heart of Manhattan. Together we stopped in at an upscale jewelry store near Central Park and picked out a modest gold band. The ring was etched with small stars and stripes, and we both knew it was the perfect choice. Again she humored me, when right there in front of the jeweler, I got down again on bended knee and slid the diamond ring onto her delicate finger, then scooped her up and carried her over the store's threshold and out into the perfect afternoon.

I knew Elizabeth was thrilled about the proposal, but she seemed a bit preoccupied when I set her down, almost resigned. We sat on a park bench for a spell, and I couldn't help but ask her if she was okay. Was anything the matter? She reassured me this was the best day of her life, other than the day I had caught her stealing food from the mess hall. Then she turned to me and took my hand in hers. We both stared down at the diamond on her finger, sparkling as it caught the daylight.

"I'm pregnant with our baby, Henry."

Members of *Priority Gal*'s crew photographed after a mission in 1944. From left to right: Robert Krusan, navigator; Henry Supchak, pilot; William Sheppard, tail gunner; Guy La Rocco, ball turret gunner; Anthony Skorpik, waist gunner; John Karlac, copilot. (*Author*)

PART FIVE

The Search

TWENTY-FOUR

W HEN THE WAR ENDED AND ANDER'S FATHER
returned home, he was never quite the same.
His mother contracted pneumonia and died by the
time Ander was ten, so Aunt Julia took it as her
responsibility to raise Ander. Because the hut and
truck had been demolished by the plane crash and
Ander's father was unwell, the Haas family fell on
very hard times over those next several years. Slow
but sure, Ander and his aunt resurrected the sheepshearing business.

It took years, but with the help of Aunt Julia's new
husband, Jacob, the shearing hut was making money
again. The new dwelling was two stories high, held
solid by brick and mortar on the exterior, and lined
on the interior with thick wood planks of knotty

pine. Uncle Jacob and Ander would stand on the split-rail fence and dare even a rocket to try and knock this building down.

As was expected Ander had to work while his sisters attended school, but it only made him more determined than ever to get himself an education someday. One could say he lived vicariously through his sisters' schooling. He lay in bed at night and listened to them telling tales of their day, and it made him smile and sometimes giggle. They talked about mundane things, like the crabby headmaster, or the girl who let a pig into the school.

On Sundays, Ander's only day off, his sisters would read to him from their textbooks and literature books, and he couldn't get enough. The girls were certainly smart, and Ander discovered early on that he was a quick study as well. Ander knew his sisters adored him, and that made him special somehow. They also imparted an understanding of the female species into his otherwise rugged, boyish brain. Girls spent more time in the bathroom, they had more tears than boys, they liked flowers and tea parties and frilly dolls, and they didn't have to go to war.

With hard work by day and studying with his sisters at every opportunity, Ander saved his money and passed his university entrance exam. He was eager to get a real education and was grateful to his sisters for making it possible. At eighteen he left Neustift for the first time and traveled to England to study business.

In the early sixties Austria was in a tremendous economic growth spurt, tourism a primary means of business. This was right around the time Ander inherited one of the most amazing pieces of real estate in the world: a chunk of the Austrian Alps. Since shearing was no longer done there, and the two-story structure overlooking the town of Neustift was unused, Ander decided to renovate the building into a tavern on the main floor and convert the upper level to a bed and breakfast with six quaint rooms. He wanted to keep the integrity of the mountainside lodge, but enhance it. A hiking trail was cut through the brush along the ravine where Ander had shepherded for so many years. Hikers of all shapes, sizes, and nationalities made their way to the top of the mountain, if they dared to venture that far.

The split-rail fence had been restored at least three times, and benches encouraged rest stops for novice hikers. Slow and silent, the gutted ground where the bomber exploded filled in with stones over time, the ravine just as smooth and cool as when Ander first sat in it at the age of five. He recalled Aunt Julia telling him that nothing could stop water in any of its forms: wet, ice, or even steam. Ander was grateful to his Aunt Julia. He knew he loved her, but he had also grown to appreciate her as a person with wisdom and common sense. She had taught him so many things about life. He hadn't liked her constant talking when he was younger, but in retrospect—as a successful thirty-year-old entrepreneur—Ander recognized many of his ideologies and idiosyncrasies came from his Aunt Julia.

Things were going well for Ander, and then he met Christine, and his world changed in ways he never imagined. Christine was a singer with a voice that could melt a man's heart, and she had done just that to Ander. Married in a small chapel in Neustift, they invited half the town to the reception, which was thrown in the best inn in town.

The village of Neustift at the base of those Alps had been through hell during World War II. By the skin of its teeth Neustift survived, and the townsfolk, including Ander and his boys, rallied together over the years and rebuilt the hamlet into an international tourist attraction. It didn't take long for him to realize that he had the golden touch.

When he was a child, Ander envied the folks who lived in the three large estates at the base of the Alps. He and Aunt Julia passed them on their trek to and from the shearing hut every day, and Ander had studied the warm glow that emanated from within. When the weather was warm, his aunt always made a big fuss over the flower-adorned baskets that hung from all the window sills on the estates. All my favorite colors, she'd exclaim, each day pointing out a new shade, never a dead one in the bunch. When Ander turned forty, he and Christine purchased the three estates.

Renovations to the structures on the inside, while trying to maintain the authenticity on the exterior,

The Alpensporthotel, Neustifterhof, built by Ander Haas near the site of his family's original sheepshearing building, which was destroyed in *Priority Gal's* crash. (*Ander Haas*)

proved time consuming and costly. The project took several years, but by 1985 all three estates had been transformed into Tyrolean inns—the best in the Stubai Valley. Ander hired his sons, now out of college, to work as managers.

Over the next several years Christine would give birth to a brood of Tyrolean children, all raised on the upper level of the central inn, the most glorious of the three, as far as Christine was concerned. It was a bucolic setting to raise a family, and the Haas children were quite fortunate, but Ander knew the importance of teaching his children the same work ethic by which he had been raised.

Aside from spending time with his family, one of Ander's favorite activities—and something he did every day without fail unless the temperature was dangerously cold—was to hike to the top of the glacier and then back down. It took a few hours, but that was a luxury of owning his own businesses, and he made time to hike every day. When he was a teenager, he hiked to the shearing hut and back because Aunt Julia had drilled into his head that only the addlepated drove in such a majestic place. Ander believed that if he stopped walking, he'd stop living.

Eventually, he figured out that if he built something on the top of the mountain, he himself could enjoy a relaxing respite before heading back down the mountain. His idea was to build another pub at the top of the mountain for food, schnapps, and lager. Since hiking after drinking at high altitudes was never a good thing, Ander invested with a couple of other Austrian businessmen in a means of transportation, both up and down the mountain, in the form of a gondola service. Tourists could enjoy the gorgeous scenery from above or from the ground.

Adjacent to the pub at the top, Ander later built a sporting goods depot, equipped with everything one possibly needed for survival on a glacier. Ander's routine involved stopping at his bed and breakfast for a quick greeting to the pub caretaker, then he continued the trek. It was the same routine on the way down, only he'd occasionally grab a shot of Umblachter, a sharp Austrian liquor.

One glorious spring afternoon, on his way back down the mountain, Ander stopped along the split-rail fence and hopped up to sit as he had done many years ago with his aunt. A few goats roamed around along the stream's edge, and he marveled at how so much was different and yet so very little had changed. He liked to reminisce about his life in the Alps. He thought of the last time he and Aunt Julia had been together, sitting along that fence.

Before Aunt Julia passed away a few years back, Ander had taken her up to the shearing hut after it had been transformed into a bed and breakfast with all the accoutrements. "All the bells and whistles," as she put it. She wouldn't tell him she was impressed with the whole concept, but he knew she was proud for both of them. They shared the notion that the shearing business they struggled to hang onto all those years had made way for newness and growth.

Like so many years before, the two sat side by side on a bench overlooking the ravine. It was then Aunt Julia told him that the bomber that crashed in 1944 was buried under all that rubble in the ravine. She recollected for Ander that when the Germans came up the dirt road a few days after the crash, she was in the burned brush looking for sheep that may have survived. While hiding, she watched from a distance as a huge machine dug a deep hole and shoved all the debris in and buried it. She gestured to the exact spot from where they sat. She claimed to be comforted by the parts resting there, sort of like secret buried treasure.

Ander was stunned at this information. He had never even considered there were pieces of the bomber left, remnants of history buried right there on his property all these years. He was six when that man had risked his life to prevent the plane from wiping out his village. After learning this new information, the idea of bomber parts buried in the Alps never left his thoughts for too long.

Sitting there alone on the fence, he had a suspicion there was something he was missing. There were no messages from above, no ghosts to tell him what to do next. He knew what the next logical step would be. The rudiments of Ander's next venture were already taking shape.

TWENTY-FIVE

ANYONE LOOKING IN FROM THE OUTSIDE WOULD swear I was the luckiest guy in the neighborhood. I had an amazing wife; smart, healthy children; a dog; and even a white picket fence. I involved myself in my kids' activities, school projects, and baseball coaching throughout the course of their childhoods. I built a backyard playhouse for my daughter, replete with shingles and furniture. I put in a swimming pool and taught my kids all sorts of things, from astronomy to zoology. We went on kid-friendly vacations every year and enjoyed the splendors and decadence of holidays.

For over twenty years I was employed as a process engineer for Ford Motor Company, where I earned enough money to pay off a house and put my kids through college. Elizabeth and I together made a handsome income, and when the children were grown, we traveled all over the world. At some point we vacationed in Austria, and while touring Innsbruck, I didn't have the nerve to tell Elizabeth that the town less than a mile from the inn where we were staying was the exact spot I landed when I bailed out so many years before. She'd convince me to go and have closure, or some such nonsense, and I preferred to let it be.

We were a patriotic family, with a flagpole on our front lawn. Elizabeth was even more so than I. She always saw the good in this country, in the government, in the people. Unfortunately, I had become somewhat of a cynic. Sure, I loved this country, but I harbored a resentment I couldn't put my finger on. I continued to have long periods of time when I didn't want any human contact. I could be triggered into a depression by one of my kids simply whining the declaration as kids do, "I'm starving." Unless they went days without food, I resented them using the word. It seemed silly, but very real. Wasting food was another one of my triggers. Perhaps that was the underlying reason I chose food services as my air force assignments after the war.

I avoided watching war movies, even *Twelve O'Clock High* and *The Great Escape*. *Hogan's Heroes* was avoided, and that was a popular comedy. Much of my behavior, though explainable, didn't feel right. Since returning home, I had yet to talk about my war experiences with anyone. I wanted people to know, so they would understand, but then if they understood, they wouldn't ask about it. Elizabeth knew only what I shared with her when we first met. She knew it had been bad, but there were images too disturbing for her to have to visualize, and I spared her those details. If she asked me a direct question, I answered with the truth. The topic was never one I brought up with anyone.

Early on, my daughter Izzy, upon learning that one of her kindergarten classmate's father was in jail for domestic abuse, proudly announced to her class that her father had been a prisoner, too. Of course the teacher assumed I had been arrested, but when I asked Izzy where she heard that I was a prisoner, she said she'd heard me have bad dreams. The further away from the war, the deeper went my suppressed memories. During the day I could keep them at bay, but they wreaked havoc on my nights. There was no safe distance from the war without totally losing oneself.

When I retired from the automotive industry with a decent pension, it allowed me the luxury of finally going back to school. A bachelor's degree was something you were supposed to earn while you still were one, but I didn't pay attention to naysayers. I wanted to earn a college degree. When I was in high school back in Nanticoke, I never imagined my life would be derailed from college. I had earned a few credits from a local community college when Pearl Harbor was attacked. I enlisted the next day. I figured I'd resume school when I got home.

The first class I took was a basic English class. I had always harbored a deep appreciation for the written word, and since it had been over a half a century that I received a lesson in grammar, I figured college English was as good a place as any to start.

Needless to say I was the oldest in the class. The first assignment was to write an essay in the first person about anything. Sounded simple enough, until I sat with pencil in hand and the scene that kept coming to mind was my bailout. Elizabeth convinced me it would be good therapy, so I wrote. I kept on writing. I went as far back as I could remember, and in chronological order I wrote the story of my life.

After I began the journey of writing my story, it became easier to talk about it. My son-in-law, Jimmy, was the first one to ask about my war experiences besides Elizabeth—really ask out of genuine interest. My own kids were probably subliminally taught to fear asking me anything as it may upset me. Jimmy sat enamored, and the more he encouraged me to go on, the more I told him. He said there were a lot of people in the world who would appreciate hearing about my experiences, especially the POW part.

Under pressure from Elizabeth, I got up the nerve to accept invitations to talk to my grandkids' school assemblies. I spoke at Memorial Day parades and

Veteran's Day ceremonies. My topic in my talks was always consistent: freedom. I even joined the local VFW and began using the regional VA hospital for some of my medical needs. It didn't seem to matter how much I talked about my life in the military—following what the experts recommended by getting it all out in the open—the mild but persistent nagging continued.

Over the years I had surgeries on my knees and frostbitten toes and developed war-related ailments, but the worst was the lesion within, causing the nightmares. I would wake up drenched in cold sweat, bolt upright, startling Elizabeth awake. She would hold me until my heart was a safe distance from stroke level, and then we'd cry. This went on throughout the entire marriage. At times of stress, of course, it was always more frequent.

I was honored with a variety of service medals over the years, as various committees decided to recognize something they hadn't noticed before. When my story became public locally, my son-in-law had been right. The POW experience was intriguing to folks. Here was Jimmy, a carefree guy, encouraging me to brag about my war experiences. I improved over time in the telling of my story, from "maggot soup to nuts," as I referred to the whole story. The more I told it, the easier it was to tell a little more each time. Still, there was that damn lingering foreboding that I just couldn't shake. All this closure bullshit should have been making me feel unburdened and relieved, but instead I was experiencing more nightmares and insomnia than ever before.

One night in 1981 I dreamt about my crew. I had dreamt of them before, but this time it was a new dream, and they were all dead. I woke with a start. By not staying in contact with my men, had I deserted them?

TWENTY-SIX

I DECIDED TO BEGIN MY SEARCH FOR THE CREW OF *Priority Gal* by emptying my footlocker, the one sent home when I didn't return to base on July 31, 1944. It remained unopened for years in my parent's attic and then was moved to my crawl space after they had passed away. Opening up the footlocker was not going to be easy, but I had no choice if I wanted to get the full names and addresses of all my crew members from back in the forties. It was as good a place as any to start, and all I had was time since retiring.

I dragged the military-issued trunk out of its dark, dank space, and in the light of day my black stenciled named stared up at me, *Lieutenant Henry W. Supchak*. It took a screwdriver to pry open the rusted latch, but eventually it popped, and the hinges yawned and creaked as I opened the lid. A nostalgia came over me when the antiquated smells wafted from within.

I had always been a fastidious type, and I was grateful the contents were in neat order. There were folded uniforms and flight suits, along with a few caps and socks and underwear, an unopened box of bullets for my Colt, and other military paraphernalia. Papers were stacked neatly with a few magazines from the era. On the very bottom of the trunk was a folder tagged "Crew," and inside the folder was a small bio on each member of *Priority Gal*'s crew. I spent a while looking at six or seven black-and-white photos of all of us before prison camp. In good health, they had been an amazing bunch of brave men, indeed. It made me more determined to find each one of them.

Granted, the information in the folder was almost forty years old, but it was all I had to go on. I went to the public library and requested a phone book for Boston. Karlac would be the first one on my list, since Elizabeth and I were traveling to California on a spring vacation, and she had arranged for a six-hour layover in Massachusetts. When I located a number for him, Elizabeth made the call to ascertain whether Karlac still lived there. He did.

The door to Karlac's brownstone in downtown east Boston was answered by a lovely, unassuming woman, Bernice, who introduced herself as the housekeeper and showed us to a study. Well, a study, I mused. Karlac really was a snob. I glanced about the room, at the book-lined shelves, the art pieces and artifacts adorning this room, and knew Karlac and I were from very different worlds.

When the doors to the study opened, I watched as a man in a wheelchair whirled his way into the room. Before I could utter a word, Karlac exclaimed, "I know, I know. I look awfully like a copilot of yours, only the other guy could walk." He laughed, and all the while his body trembled. "Parkinson's, sir. Do I still have to call you that?" He didn't wait for an answer. He gestured to his chair. "Don't worry, it's not contagious, and I won't suffer long."

"Lieutenant Karlac. Good to see you." I gave him my best salute. "How have you been?"

"Well, other than experiencing life as a 'bitter party of one' since returning to the states in '45, I think my life is peachy. Oh, did I mention? I have Parkinson's disease." He wheeled over to a corner wet bar that I hadn't noticed and made himself a drink. "How did your life turn out? You look trim and healthy, always did." He sighed. "I always resented the way the crew liked you so much. They had no respect for me, I knew that. But I did the missions same as you, and I did prison camp same as you. Put in my time, same as you, but you got the Distinguished Flying Cross, and I got shit."

I recalled that being one of Karlac's favorite words. "The medals mean nothing to me compared to my freedom," I responded. "You should be happy to be alive and still have your faculties about you. You became an attorney, right? Isn't that something to be proud of?"

"It took me six tries to pass the bar," he chortled. "I believe if it weren't for the war, I'd be walking around, probably playing golf or tennis right now. But I'm crippled, or whatever the politically correct word is these days—disabled, handicapped, challenged. I almost wish this *was* a war injury, and then I'd have a real excuse to hate life and blame someone else."

I was having a tough time listening to him, and I told him it was time to move on, like *I* was some sort of expert. "You need to forget about the war, Karlac."

"With all due respect, if you want me to forget about the war, then why the hell are you here?"

Back out in the car, Elizabeth saw me coming down Karlac's walkway and gently placed her bookmark between the pages of a library book and closed it. "How did it go?" she asked after I was in my seat.

"Not so good." I leaned my head back on the driver's side headrest and sighed. "This is a lot harder than I thought." As soon as the words escaped my mouth, I already knew what was coming.

"Nothing ventured, nothing gained."

I hoped my visit with Michael Hettler, *Priority Gal's* first radio operator, went better than my time with Karlac. Hettler lived in Delaware, and on a solo trip to visit my youngest son, Steven, in North Carolina, I decided to stop by and see him.

He lived on a modest lot, maybe an acre, with a small cottage at the back of the property. It was very quaint and comfortable. He had iced tea and lemonade prepared, and we sat and talked about life after the war. His face was so mutilated on the one side, and thus I understood when he told me he rarely ventured out. He was fortunate his parents left him this little piece of property and the cottage. He never married, so there were no children. In the past few years he had developed hepatitis B, and was waiting on a liver transplant that he didn't believe would come to fruition.

Somehow the conversation came around to music, and we hit on a positive chord. When the subject of the violin came up, his tragically scarred face lit up. I told him how I had learned to play a little violin over the years but just never got around to taking lessons.

"It's never too late, you know, sir."

We sat quiet for a while after that, enjoying the sounds of birds and breezes in his well-manicured yard. Suddenly he stood, asked to be excused a moment, and went inside. The sound of the screen door slamming behind him startled me, and I hoped my visit hadn't upset him.

When he reemerged from the house, he held a satchel, which I recognized immediately.

"Well, I'll be damned, Hettler. You still have it." I was astonished. "Is that really the same violin?"

"Yes, sir, same violin." He proudly removed it from the velvet sheath and held it as if it were an injured pet. "I never got around to repairing the hole and the strings on it, or maybe I just wanted to keep it the way it was. I don't really know." He stared down at the delicate instrument. The bow was still snapped where the bullet had passed through it, living proof of what saved Hettler's life. Unfortunately, his face bore the scars of survival.

"You know, I didn't find out until years later through some 323rd Bomb Group newsletter about the fate of *Priority Gal*. That you guys had been shot down and became POWs. I was in the hospital for months after I got hit. I had over a thousand splinters removed from my head. Had to have six units of blood, guess one of the units was sick."

He paused and took a long swallow of lemonade. He poured us both more, and by the gesture I knew he intended for me to visit a little longer, so I did.

"You know," he continued as he put down the dripping pitcher, "surgeon said if I hadn't had the bow to break the trajectory of the bullet, it would have hit me right between the legs instead. The doctor said how lucky I was. I could still have children." He laughed and I heard the irony in his tone. "Who's going to want to have children with a guy who looks like me?"

"You're a brave airman, Hettler, and don't let anyone kid you. Women love a man in uniform, with or without a head." This time Hettler had a hardy laugh, and it did my heart good.

"You know, Hank. I can call you Hank?"

I nodded.

"I always used the fact that *Priority Gal* was shot down to rationalize that what happened to me had to be better than what happened to you guys. Look at you, though, no worse for the wear. Makes me wonder."

"War is horrendous, Hettler. You got scars on the outside, I got scars on the inside. It's just an ugly situation." Who was I to judge which was worse, his injuries or my loss of freedom?

"Do you ever regret your time served?" he asked.

In all the years since coming home, I had never really looked at the months I spent in prison camp as something to regret. Regret, to me, suggested something I could have done differently, something I could have prevented. I had little control over my situation, and I survived. "No," I responded. "No regrets."

Hettler gently returned the violin and broken bow to the satchel, leaned forward, and placed it on my lap. "I want you to have this, sir." His eyes were brimming with tears, and I was at a loss. "It's my way of saying thanks for getting me home alive on all twenty-two missions we had together."

He must have seen the hesitation and confusion in my expression.

"Let's be honest. I really don't have anyone . . . no one who has any appreciation for the instrument. I know you will take good care of it. Restring it, bury this bow and get a new bow. Take lessons. Please, take it."

What could I say? I graciously accepted his offering, and when I left that day, I reassured him it was in loving hands. We embraced and I saw more of his tears.

TWENTY-SEVEN

Retired Chief Glenn Thomas lived alone in a small clapboard home in Delaware off a major interstate highway. We sat in his kitchen over mugs of coffee, and he told me about his world since the war. He was a cross-country trucker for numerous companies and had saved enough money to buy his own rig. He gave me a short tour of the cab, and I saw a picture of a girl in a Santa hat I assumed to be the daughter he talked of back in '44.

Turns out, his baby girl was gone when he arrived back home to Wilmington in the summer of 1945. His wife had married another man, believing when he went missing in action that he must have been dead. By the time he saw his wife again, she was already six months pregnant with her new husband's baby. Thomas went back in the air force and became a lifer, retiring at forty-five with full benefits and half his pay for the rest of his life. He claimed he never ran into any of the guys from *Priority Gal's* crew, not since Camp Lucky Strike.

Following retirement from military service, he pursued his lifelong dream of driving around the country on someone else's dollar. He had married twice, twice divorced, and only saw his daughter on Christmas afternoons. I noticed he wasn't unhappy. There had been a much overdue mellowing of his personality from when I last saw him forty years earlier. He had gone a little soft in his old age, but hadn't we all?

It was becoming increasingly difficult for me to accept that some of the crew had not gotten the decent life they deserved. I had received a tremendous amount of attention for my military service over the years, but I never relied on it. Thomas relied on the military to define him, and that may have been a mistake. All in all he was, for the most part, content—a roof over his head, a paycheck, and a grown daughter out there somewhere, even if he only saw her once a year.

In 1985, acquiescing to Elizabeth's suggestions once again, we flew to Chicago to attend my first official POW convention. The whole idea of a convention to me was ridiculous, and brought to mind salesmen and politicians. This was a gathering of all sorts of formerly imprisoned men—injured and damaged men. I wondered if they had nightmares like I did.

I located the area where the 91st Bomb Group had a table and was surprised after a few minutes to run into Rocco, Skorpik, Taylor, and Sheppard. These former enlisted crew members seemed to be managing their lives very well. They all had gone on to have families, kids, and grandkids. We talked about Leahy, his premature death not surprising anyone. We all knew he had gotten the worst blow in prison camp. I caught them up on the lives of Karlac, Hettler, and Thomas. The only crew members left were Feinman and Krusan.

These four guys had been coming to these conventions for the past twenty years. Rocco said it was because of the free food—but I knew better. They had come to terms with their pasts; I was just starting. Maybe it was true that the best therapy was being around those who experienced similar misery. We talked about nightmares and so much more. Only the soldiers who were coping with their issues could attend such an event, I figured. That idea made me feel good about myself. The discussions and emotional bonding went on until the wee hours of the morning.

We spent time reminiscing about our pasts, and gaining some idea what we had sacrificed for our country. I had to admit to Elizabeth, and to myself, on the return trip to New Jersey that I had enjoyed myself at the convention and even felt a real sense of closure this time. I thanked my wife wholeheartedly for being there with me at every turn—waiting patiently in the room at the convention, or in the car, or sometimes coming in with me.

Her response: "cause I love you."

Feinman had been from New York State, so I did a little homework and found his address in a jeweler directory, recalling his father had been a big-time diamond seller in the city. I found enough to trace him to a small town near Poughkeepsie. I was wary to meet up with Feinman because I never got an answer at his home when I telephoned. I left messages, but he never returned them. I couldn't imagine he'd still be mad at me after all these years, but so far I wasn't having the best of luck with my reunions. The enlisted guys were great, but the officers were worse off than I was, and I was pursuing them so I could heal my wounds.

Outside Feinman's supposed old address, Elizabeth waited in the car this time as well. When I knocked on the door, a younger man answered. He looked a lot like Feinman had years back.

"Can I help you?" the young man asked.

"Hello, I'm looking for Stewart Feinman." I knew this man had to be a relative of the Feinman I once knew and couldn't believe my good fortune. The man hesitated, then stepped onto the porch, and closed the door behind him.

"Did you know my father? Are you the man leaving messages?" He didn't sound angry, just curious.

"Yes, yes, I did know your father." I was encouraged. "Name's Supchak, Lieutenant Supchak. Perhaps he may have mentioned me? We served in WWII together and I—well, I wanted to see how he was managing."

"I'm sorry. Stewart Feinman was my father, but he passed away last year. Cancer."

I felt the prickle of tears forming in my eyes.

"My dad never talked about the war," he offered. "We knew it affected him because he had long stretches of time when he would shut down, then he'd have scream dreams, my mother and I came to calling them after a while. He'd wake half the apartment building. As a kid I knew something was wrong, but I had no idea what it was. It was really just a few months before he died that he told us he wanted forgiveness from the family rabbi over regrets from World War II." The man looked upward as if trying to prevent tears of his own from rolling down his cheeks. "Sorry, I'm going on and on. It's just that we knew he was hurting, but we assumed holding it in was less painful than talking about it. We were wrong, of course."

"I'm so sorry for your loss." I meant it too. I felt that familiar lump rise like yeast in my throat and figured I'd better hightail it back to the safety net of Elizabeth. "Your father was a brave and decent man—funny, too." I wanted him to know how I felt about his dad, the little I knew of Lieutenant Stewart Feinman.

"I appreciate you saying that, Mr. Supchak." He brushed the tears from his cheeks with his sleeve, and I saw the little boy inside the man that he was trying to be, strong for his father, but unable to hold it in sometimes. Before he turned back to the door to open it and disappear behind it, I extended my hand to wish him the best and asked, "I'm sorry, what did you say your name was?"

"Henry, sir, Henry Feinman."

TWENTY-EIGHT

KRUSAN PROVED THE MOST DIFFICULT TO TRACK down. Karlac hadn't seen him, and Feinman was gone. I was able to find Krusan's wife by her maiden name. Somehow I remembered it—Bordeaux—and sure enough a relative of Sally's was in the telephone book. Krusan was still alive, but just barely. He had brittle type II diabetes and late stages of congestive heart failure. When Sally Bordeaux Krusan found out who I was, she begged me to come and visit her husband. She said she didn't think he'd be around too much longer; his prognosis was poor, and she refused to accept no for an answer.

My old friend, Lieutenant Krusan, was in a La-Z-Boy recliner attached to a green oxygen tank. He had been a heavy smoker, as I recalled. He was bloated, and the skin on his arms was shades of mottled purple.

As hard as we both tried to speak, when his eyes met mine for the first time, we just shook our heads and smiled through tears. I sat down next to him and grabbed his swollen, bruised hand. He leaned in to me and kept saying, "son of a bitch, sir, *son of a bitch.*"

When we finally pulled it together, we laughed at our weepy, schoolgirlish behavior, and then got down to business.

"I never in a million years figured on seeing your ugly mug again." Krusan looked me over. "You look damn good for a guy who spent a year starving in prison camp."

"I still have my full set of teeth—now that says something, doesn't it?"

"Yeah, Supchak, sir. You can thank your Polish hardheadedness." He seemed glad as hell to see me, maybe as much as I was grateful to see him.

I decided to come out and ask. "So, Kruz, tell me what it was like when you heard about *Priority Gal's* fate?" I didn't realize it until just then, sitting side by side again with my navigator, how desperately I needed his perspective on the events of July 31, 1944, besides having breakfast together.

"Well, the truth of the matter was, right after I left the mess hall, I grabbed a local paper and read it from front to back and then fell sound asleep. Remember, I had a little too much bad whiskey during poker the night before. So I'm taking a nap, and I get startled awake by Gumbo, who said I needed to go see Commander Terry. Given our risky business—bombs at twenty-eight thousand feet and all—I'm surprised it never once dawned on me that something had happened to *Priority Gal*."

Krusan's wife came into the room with cans of beer and shots of whiskey. He affectionately tapped her rear end. "Isn't she the greatest? I tell her she needs to find another man. Who wants to be a Winston widow, huh?" He coughed through gurgles.

"Kids?" I asked his wife, changing the subject away from death by cigarettes.

She walked over to a side bar and picked up a set of connected photos, three black-and-white pictures of two girls and a boy. "Three," she said. "All grown up now."

"Me too." I took a few seconds to admire the pictures and then handed them back to Sally. She put the frame back in its place and silently retreated from the room, leaving us alone again.

"Bout time she left," he winked at me. He downed his shot. "*Ahhhhh*," he gave a satisfied groan. "She's a good woman. Too good for the likes of me, what can I say? She gets me. That's what I love about her."

"She's quite lovely." I didn't know how to respond. I knew he wasn't an easy fellow to get. None of us veterans were at that point.

He went on, ignoring the last five minutes of the awkward conversation he had just generated. I was relieved he returned to answering my question.

"Anyway, that day—what was it, a Monday? Yeah, it was a Monday because poker was Sunday nights. So

I'm standing in Terry's office, and he tells me straight up without mincing any words, something to the effect that they're all MIA in enemy territory." Krusan ran his hand over his lumpy, balding scalp. "*Whew!* When I heard that, I dropped into the nearest chair. I was in shock."

I could tell he didn't like talking about it, but I knew if I didn't hear it now I would never know. Besides, Krusan was a strong man in spite of all his medical ailments. He had a great heart, and maybe it was healthy for him to talk about it. Who else would care that he was the one left behind?

"When I got my wits about me again, I convinced myself you guys would be okay. You had our asses up at night twice a week practicing. We knew that bailout routine like we knew how to breathe and so on and so on. I convinced myself you were alive. Then I felt this impulse to protect you. The first thing I did was bolt from Terry's office to your bunk. I wanted to be sure the footlocker that got sent home to Mom and Pop didn't have a pornographic calendar, or something else unsavory in the family's eyes—you know how it was. Of course, they now have a name for the likes of you. With all due respect, sir, 'anal retentive' ring any bells?" This time when he laughed he began to cough, and I wondered if he was going to catch his breath. He did and cursed his lungs, but not the cigarettes.

"I got the footlocker back, so thanks." I knew that when planes went down and crews didn't return, if no one packed up your belongings, the footlocker would sooner than later get ransacked, and there would be nothing left. I assumed it was why my copilot was calling over the radio to get his dry cleaning. If it sat at the dry cleaners too long, they assumed he wouldn't be returning anytime soon—if ever—and they sold or kept the clothes.

"That had to be strange to open the trunk for the first time in all those years." He looked quizzically at me for a reaction.

"I didn't open it—not at first. I stashed it in an attic in my parent's house, where it sat for several decades. You're right, though, opening that trunk latched shut since 1944 was quite a surreal experience." Like a blast from the past, and not necessarily a welcome one. "The good thing to come from delving into my harrowing past was that I found the full names and original addresses for *Priority Gal*'s crew. I made the decision then and there to find out where you men were. I started two years ago and saved the best for last. That'd be you, Krusan."

"Oh, I see. So you think if you butter me up, I'm going to give you some sort of welcome gift? Do ya?" He smiled broadly. From behind his back he produced a small brown package, the size of a five-and-dime novel. The wrapping was neat and tied up with a white string like a miniature bakery box. He handed it to me.

"What's this?" I hesitated before taking it, as though he were hiding one of those toy buzzers in his palm. "Should I open it?" I asked, and knew I sounded ridiculous.

"No. Save it till I'm dead, so I don't get any satisfaction out of seeing your smiling, appreciative face."

"Always the greatest at sarcasm. It actually becomes you, Krusan." I looked back down at the lightweight package. "Okay, okay, I'll open it." I fumbled with the string, feeling a little self-conscious. The brown paper fell away easily, and I held a small log in my hands. I knew, without seeing, what this little book was all about. This little diary told the very brave and patriotic story of *Priority Gal*. Krusan was giving me his official handwritten logbook detailing each and every mission—except of course, my last.

"I heard through the grapevine you were writing a book, and I figured this has good information. I hope it helps."

I was touched by the gift, but furious with Elizabeth. Writing a book, was she kidding? Sure, I was happy to get whatever information I could to finish my memoirs, but a book?

Krusan cleared his throat. "You want to know what really got me? I had to take my last flight with a group of novice jockos I'd never met before, better yet flown with. It was probably the most anticlimactic experience of my life." He took a sip of his beer. "I ended up going home alone. I should have been celebrating, but I was on a plane surrounded by crews of guys who all seemed to know each other."

"I thought about you when I was captured. I knew you were going to take it hard." Although I would rather have been going home than remain in prison camp, I can imagine the emptiness Krusan must have felt. "I wished you'd been in camp with us for the laughs, Kruz. We missed you." I gave him a broad facetious smile.

He laughed. "Hey, I had a terrible sense of guilt that I wasn't with you guys. I know it was no shits and giggles—it was prison. But all in all I never felt lucky I wasn't there. Isn't that strange?"

"You're a true hero and a gentleman. I mean that, Krusan." He had a certain luck on his side in choosing that flight to miss, and should be proud he completed all his assigned missions. "You're the only one of us who didn't get caught."

When it was time for me to say goodbye, I leaned down and hugged my friend. "See you on the other side," I whispered in his ear. I stood erect gave him my best salute and headed toward the door. I knew there would be a parting shot—there always was from Lieutenant Bob Krusan.

"Ya know," he said quizzically, "did you ever consider the fact that if I had been on that mission you would have made the Swiss border and never been a POW?"

"Thought about that every day in prison camp, my friend." I closed his front door behind me as tears blurred my vision.

TWENTY-NINE

I GUESS IT COULD BE SAID THAT I WAS A PIONEER IN a long succession of military family members. I officially retired from the air force in 1960, after nearly twenty years of loyal service. Elizabeth served in the Korean War as a MASH nurse. My oldest son, Paul, attended the Naval Academy and went on to fly the prestigious F/A-18 for the Marine Corps, earning Top Gun and Tail Hook medals. My youngest son, Steven, started out as a marine, the only member of the family to survive the infamous Parris Island. He then went on to a full career with the United States Coast Guard, retiring with high honors.

There was one special person I wanted to believe I had influenced in a positive way, and that was my son-in-law, Jimmy. As soon as my daughter brought him home, he and I shared a passion for airplanes and rockets. He told me he wanted to fly ever since he could remember. At the time we had our early conversations, when Jimmy had hair halfway down his back and a bohemian sort of attitude and grilled me about my war experiences—for whatever reason, I enjoyed his company.

Jimmy cut his hair and joined the Marine Corps in 1980 while still in college with my daughter at Villanova University. His goal was to graduate from Officer Candidate School in Quantico, Virginia, then head to Pensacola for flight school. He did all that, and somewhere in the middle of it all, on my sixty-sixth birthday, he married my daughter, Izzy.

For the next few years Jimmy succeeded in getting assigned to jets—a 1 percent shot. After traveling with my daughter and, soon enough, their two baby sons all over the country, he eventually transferred to the navy to fly the A-6 Intruder out of Chase Naval Air Base in Virginia Beach. Just as I was of my own two sons, I was proud of my son-in-law—and he knew it.

A year into his new assignment in 1986 he was deployed to a carrier off the coast of Libya; Muammar Gaddafi was rearing his ugly head for the first time. On a mission Jimmy's right engine caught fire, and the plane went down. Neither Jimmy nor the copilot survived the crash.

I took his death hard—not only because my daughter and their two boys had lost a husband and father, but because Jimmy was my buddy. I respected him and how far he had gone in his quest to fly, from frat boy in college to the benevolent warrior. He had died doing what he loved, but it still hurt. I recall a point where I said to Elizabeth that I wished it had been me. How the hell was I allowed to survive all that crap forty years earlier, and this poor guy with a young wife and two infant sons was now a statistic?

Elizabeth, always the word of reason, said if I had died forty years ago, we would have never had Izzy, and none of this would be happening. We needed to be there for Izzy and her two babies. If anything, we had an amazingly supportive family during those rough times, and everyone came to the aid of my daughter. I, on the other hand, made it my personal mission to help with the two little boys. They no longer had a father, but I could be a decent male role model. It was a legacy I was fortunate enough to have. So much in the world is fragile, and so much can change in an instant. No one knew that better than I did.

The culmination of my military career came in 2004, when along with twenty some odd members of my family, I attended the unveiling of the World War II Memorial in our nation's capital. It was held over Memorial Day weekend that year, and the weather in Washington, DC, was perfect. Cherry blossoms rained everywhere, and it was one of the first times I was a part of a war-related event in which I didn't feel sadness. This time I felt pride—pride in my country, pride in my men, and pride in myself.

At the entrance of the National Air and Space Museum, my nephew discovered to our surprise that my name was engraved on one of the silver plaques lining the walkway honoring recipients of the Distinguished Flying Cross. When complete strangers came over to me and asked if I minded having my photo taken with them, I had to admit this acknowledgment felt really nice.

About a month after the trip to Washington, I learned from a POW newsletter that Hettler had passed away. From the chair in my home office, where I sat while reading the sad news, I could see Hettler's violin hanging on my wall over my desk. It had been hanging there since the day I brought it home. As much as I wanted to try my hand again at the violin, I never refurbished Hettler's instrument. This violin held a significant memory I wanted to keep. Leaving it in its original form felt more honorable.

The bow was another story altogether. A few times a year, the local VFW had a flag-burning ceremony. If you had a tattered flag, you could take it a local post, where it would be ceremoniously and respectfully burned. The flags' ashes were then sprinkled all over the country. I made a decision to attend the next flag-burning ceremony and contribute Hettler's bow in his honor. That bow had saved his life, whether he always believed in it or not. I believed the broken bow deserved a respectful military send-off. As the bow snapped and crackled in the fire can, I said a fond farewell to *Priority Gal*'s loyal radioman.

Encouraged by Elizabeth, I continued to write my memoirs. I sometimes spent several hours a day writing the story of my life. I had over a thousand handwritten pages when I finally reached the end. There was nothing more I could say about my life. Elizabeth, the war, prison camp, my crew, my childhood—it was all there on those lines on the pages.

After reaching out to the crew and then journaling it, I felt the sense of unease unwind a bit—but I continued to have unsettling thoughts. I was still missing something. Maybe this really was the end, as close as I could get to lessening my anxiety.

THIRTY

Ander Haas had no idea where to even begin looking for the man who fell from the sky back in 1944. It was ridiculous to believe the pilot was still alive. By then he'd have to be in his late eighties. Still, he had to at least try to find him. He thought back and tried to picture the man's face. He wondered if he'd recognize the American flyer. Almost sixty years later, there was no way the man would recognize Ander.

In the scheme of things Ander decided to tackle the tangible: excavation of the ravine. Most of the remains were charred, but there were a few chunks that looked like an engine and maybe a fuselage. Regardless of the cost, Ander had several intact—albeit dented and damaged—plane parts transported down to the main inn, where he had them profession-ally cleaned and identified for authenticity. He now knew beyond a shadow of a doubt that it was the real thing—but that was just the start of the puzzle. There was so much more to find out.

Ander hired historian Dr. Jakob Mayer, known for his expertise in all matters of air combat in World War II, to assist with his plan. Dr. Mayer was indeed able to identify the pieces as part of a Boeing B-17G bomber, or what was known as the Flying Fortress. Ander could understand why it had earned such a formidable name. Dr. Mayer was given the daunting assignment of locating whatever bits of information he could find about the pilot of that B-17.

Meanwhile, Ander waited for what seemed like weeks before he heard from the historian again. The good news finally came: the name of the bomber was *Priority Gal*, and the pilot taken POW was Lieutenant Henry Supchak. The bad news: it placed Supchak's age around ninety years old. What were the odds—after all the man had gone through—that he was still alive? Ander didn't bother with the odds. He needed to find out.

In 2004, Dr. Mayer emailed and posted to numerous military sites, requesting any information on Lieutenant Supchak, pilot of *Priority Gal*. He utilized such well-established Internet sites as the 91st Bomb Group, the Eighth Air Force, POW organizations, but also scoured online newspaper obituaries. After a year of hoping for a response, Dr. Mayer finally abandoned the search and delivered the news to the Haas family.

Still, Ander refused to be deterred from his original plans. He went ahead and had a bronze plaque made in honor of the town's hero who risked his own life to save them. There was a groundbreaking ceremony, and an Austrian news station followed the story of the unveiling of the plaque a few weeks later. Ander would have wanted nothing more than to say thank you to the pilot—Lieutenant Supchak—to shake his hand. But it wasn't meant to be.

Gene Elizabeth Supchak in her Air
Force dress uniform. (*Author*)

PART SIX

Lost

THIRTY-ONE

WHEN I TURNED NINETY IN 2006, ELIZABETH and I were fortunate enough to be living on our own in a comfortable townhouse in the beautiful northern New Jersey countryside. She had been experiencing some health problems, and I spent most of my time making sure she was taking her medication, going to the doctors' appointments, and eating and sleeping enough. I didn't know what the future held for us, but with Elizabeth nearing eighty, and me now ninety, it wasn't going to miraculously change for the better. I was a realist.

Elizabeth, on the other hand, was an idealist. Every day, while we sat across from each other during meals or just sitting, she would beg me to tell her about the past. She wanted to hear again and again about my meetings with Gregory Peck—one of her heartthrobs, she teased. She was always eager to hear the same stories over and over, and I obliged. After a while I realized she wanted to remember because her memory was failing.

She would lose herself for hours in boxes of old photos of the kids. Some days she spent writing notes to herself about simple things, like how to turn the heating unit on, how to write a check. With the eleven-year gap in our ages, it was only natural for me to go first, and I figured out she was preparing herself to be alone at some point down the road. I hated thinking about it, but I wasn't in denial. I read the obituaries, in which men twenty years younger than me were dying of old age.

Without fail, Elizabeth called me her hero. We had silly nicknames for each other, but wasn't that what marriage was supposed to be? Those little private nuances that pile up into knowing each other inside and out. We really were great together.

I recalled a psychology class I took as an older college student, and we were studying behavior theorists. Erik Erikson's stages of development were the topic of the lecture one night, and I learned Elizabeth and I were at the generativity-versus-stagnation stage—the last stage. We had both served our country first, and then each other, and eventually our kids and grandkids. I believed we had done a good job. We had much to be proud of. Neither of us ever relied on anyone else but each other, and we always came out on top. But the fact was, we were winding down. Our heydays had come and gone, and now we lived vicariously through our kids and grandkids.

Even with Elizabeth's health problems, we still lived independently, not relying on our kids for anything, or others to take care of us. Were we generative? I'd say so. First separately and then together we had lived productive lives, and our hearts were always in the right place. We lived a successful life, according to Erikson. Then why the hell did I still believe there was more I needed to do before the dirt nap?

THIRTY-TWO

ONE JUNE DAY, JUST AFTER LUNCH, ELIZABETH and I were quietly sitting across the table from each other, staring out at the deer grazing in the backyard of our home. It was such a serene scene when the mothers brought the fawns down to graze at the corn and bread I tossed their way. Birds nipped and tugged at each other to make room at the three feeders suspended from the overhang. I had come to appreciate some of the simpler things in life as I grew older. Sitting in a chair for long stretches of time watching nature outside the window was a favorite pastime of mine.

Elizabeth may have dozed off momentarily when the phone rang, and it startled both of us. At our age we didn't get many calls in the middle of the day. Izzy always called after work, and the boys usually held off calling until weekends.

I reached for the receiver and was surprised to hear Izzy's voice on the other end. My first thought came out of my mouth. "What's wrong?"

"Nothing's wrong. It's all good, Dad."

"What are you saying? Slow down. You're going at ninety miles an hour, and my brain can only move at forty." I had to remind my kids, and especially my grandkids, to speak slower. They talked behind my back about my need of a hearing device. If I could hear them whispering about me, then I didn't need hearing aids, I reasoned.

"Okay, okay, listen. I was on the computer. The Internet—"

I had to cut in. "Izzy, I know zero about the computer, don't even own one."

"Dad, you don't need to know about the computer. Anyway, I decided to do a search." She hesitated. "Never mind, just know that a man by the name of Dr. Mayer has been looking for you. He lives in Austria, and I gave him your phone number. He has a heavy Austrian accent, so please be patient. Dad, there are people in Austria who have been looking for you."

She waited, but I didn't know how to respond to that mouthful. "I have to get back to work, but I'll call you guys tonight. Please answer your phone!"

After she hung up and Elizabeth asked me what that was all about, I told her I had no idea. I figured it best not to stir the pot and get my wife all excited about some man calling from the other side of the ocean to talk to me. It was probably a prank. The Internet, or what I thought I knew of it, was full of scams and trickery.

Less than an hour had passed when the phone rang again. "Damn it, Izzy," I mumbled when the ringer made me jerk my relaxed neck around. Lifting the phone from the receiver, I was about to say, "Go back to work and call us later," when I heard a strange questioning voice saying hello.

"Hello." I said back into the receiver, and waited.

"Henry Supchak? Lieutenant Colonel Supchak?" The accented voice repeated my name a second time.

"Yes. Who is this?" My curiosity piqued.

"My name is Dr. Jakob Mayer, and I live in Innsbruck, Austria. I have been searching for the pilot of *Priority Gal* for years now, and it is my honor to be speaking to you, sir. I cannot believe my good fortune." He sighed as if a long journey had just ended.

"How did you find me, and why are you looking for me?" I was genuinely curious. Not just me, but Elizabeth was now all ears trying to understand what was being said on the other end of the phone line.

"Oh, Colonel, it's a long story, and someday very soon I will tell you everything. As I said, in short, I was searching on the computer for any information about you . . . but . . . well, considering your age . . . I mean, with all due respect, I never thought I'd actually find you, and without the Internet and e-mail, your daughter would have never seen my numerous posts and queries."

"That's my Izzy, but why me?"

"Austria has recently erected a monument in your name for your heroism in World War II. I was hired by a man by the name of Ander Haas, who, along with the town of Neustift, credits you for risking your life to steer your B-17 away from their village just before your bomber, *Priority Gal*, crashed into the Alps."

I was taken aback. I never believed anyone understood what had occurred that fateful day of July 31, 1944. My insane maneuver that should have killed me had been witnessed by someone. This was a twist I had never anticipated. Perhaps it was the reason for the unease I was experiencing all these years, and now I could be cured. No way was it that simple.

Dr. Mayer called back a few days later, announcing he had planned a visit to the United States. He would be arriving in September and would conduct a thorough interview for the history book he was compiling. But meanwhile, on behalf of the Haas family, he extended an invitation for an all-expenses-paid trip for Elizabeth and me to Austria the following summer.

Izzy was thrilled with the developments, and I had to admit there was an excitement in the air that was palpable, and I couldn't help but feel swept up in it. Neither Izzy nor I was as ecstatic as Elizabeth. In many ways this was her moment too. If it weren't for her constant encouragement to face my past experiences, none of this would have happened.

With Dr. Mayer's visit a month away, I found it difficult to contain myself. I checked our passports, visited several travel agents for information on traveling abroad, and put together some photos and narratives for his afternoon with me. I was antsy to get the whole Austrian story and find out who this Haas guy was and why he paid Mayer to locate me. Sometimes my mind went to conspiracy theories of disgruntled Nazis looking for revenge, but I usually settled back into believing it was a remarkable set of circumstances.

THIRTY-THREE

WHILE TIME PASSED SLOWLY THAT SUMMER OF 2006 prior to Dr. Mayer's trip, I continued writing and adding more details to my memoirs. It became the ideal outlet, and I hoped to pass the binders down to my children. I felt strongly about the future learning from the mistakes of the past. I was anxious to share what I had written with the Austrian historian. I was curious how the story of my maneuver with the bomber sixty plus years ago managed to be carried through decades, halfway across the world.

Early in August Dr. Mayer telephoned to confirm his visit set for September 9, just a little more than a month away. It was after that call that Elizabeth began suggesting that perhaps it would be better if I took Izzy with me to Austria. At first I was offended.

She had been with me all this time and was going to back out now, when it finally turned for the better. Through tears she explained that she didn't believe she was well enough to make the journey. The last thing she wanted to do was slow me down, hinder my experience. Nonsense, I told her. I didn't care if I had to carry her the whole way—she would be by my side. We decided to table the discussions about the trip until after Dr. Mayer's visit.

On August 11, while Elizabeth and I were watching the evening news, she said she wasn't feeling so well, a little short of breath, which happened occasionally after a large meal. She stood and said she was going to lie down.

"Don't lie flat, and use the banister going up." I frequently reminded her to hold on to something, knowing at our age how easy it was to lose one's balance.

Before she reached the stairwell I heard a loud *thud*, and when I turned around, I saw her lying on the hardwood floor and not moving. I pressed the emergency system we had installed in the house to alert the local EMT units, and I ran to her. I lifted her head in my arms and told her help was coming, but she was unresponsive, her head lolling in my arms. I buried my face in her warm neck and cried.

"Don't leave me, please don't leave me."

When the EMT workers arrived, they pulled me from my wife and took over trying to resuscitate. I contacted Izzy, who lived just a few miles down the road. Izzy and I followed the ambulance to the local hospital emergency room, where instead of being reunited with Elizabeth, we were told to wait for the doctor in a private room. It was then I knew with little uncertainty that my Elizabeth was gone. My life was irrevocably changed in that instant.

Elizabeth was buried with full honors in Brigadier General Doyle Cemetery as a veteran of the Korean War. It was a gorgeous day, and I managed to hold it together until my daughter-in-law sang "America the Beautiful" at the gravesite. I had tried to be brave, but in the end all I felt was an incredible loss. If it weren't for my kids, I am not sure I would have had the will to go on. The next few weeks were a blur. I couldn't think about anything else, but the enormity of what I once had that was my Elizabeth.

THIRTY - FOUR

Izzy had been maintaining an e-mail relationship with Dr. Mayer, so when it came time for his
September visit to New Jersey, she handled all the
plans and forced me to participate. I was despondent,
but I knew I had to go along with the visit, if for no
other reason than I owed it to Elizabeth to follow
through with the original plan.

Dr. Mayer spent a few days in New Jersey and
solicited the local newspaper to send a journalist to
my home for his interview. Although Mayer and I
had somewhat of a language barrier, we were able to
overcome it. I shared many of my war memories with
him, and it confirmed what he was able to come up
with in his investigations. First, he explained that he
was more than intrigued by *Priority Gal*, given her
combat history of fifty-two successful missions over

Germany. In the course of his research he discovered tremendous odds against an entire crew bailing out without incident, and then that same crew surviving life in prison camp. He had also learned of all the crew members' deaths other than my own. It saddened me to think that I was the only living crew member left.

I asked Dr. Mayer about the man who paid him to find me. This was when I learned about the little shepherd boy in the Alps, and the burns he sustained, and the gratitude he and his family had always felt for the pilot who steered the plane away. Ander and his aunt were the boy and young woman who snuck food and water to me in the outpost.

This was astonishing news to me. The boy who saved my life in the outpost was a man, moreover, a grandfather, and he wanted to thank me when I should be the one thanking him. If I had any doubts or hesitations about making the long journey to Austria, this last bit of information clinched the deal. I would find the courage to make the trip.

It was decided that my daughter would take her mother's place on the trip to Austria. The Haas family, along with the governor of Tyrol, decided to rededicate the monument when I made the journey the following summer. The ceremony was set for July

31, 2007. I had several months to plan the excursion, and God willing, I would remain alive to attend the celebration.

The months passed, and I felt compelled to document everything I could remember surrounding 1942 to 1945. When I ran out of one train of thought, I switched to another. Sometimes I'd find myself writing theories I had about the Big Bang or religion. I wrote about Dr. Mayer's visit and my upcoming trip to Austria. I wrote about Ander, the boy who had been looking for me all those years since.

I still couldn't deny the niggling of paranoia that crept into my psyche every so often when I imagined the trip. Maybe there would be some Messerschmitt pilots that would be none too happy to meet up with me again. I certainly didn't want to put my daughter in a situation in which sixty-year grudges toward me made our stay uncomfortable or, worse, dangerous.

Without too much fanfare, Izzy and I, passports in hand, left Newark airport on a Lufthansa flight for Munich, Germany. The flight would take at least eight hours, and I was too nervous to sleep. Izzy, on the other hand, was elated at the whole prospect of this vacation and slept like a cat. Since Jimmy had died, I couldn't recall a time when she ever took a holiday or vacation without her boys. For her this was a real treat, and she brought along enough luggage for a month. I couldn't help but smile when I remembered the overpacking Elizabeth was famous for doing.

Henry Supchak and his daughter Elizabeth Hoban prepare to depart for Austria. (*Authors*)

I didn't sleep on the plane and couldn't quiet my thoughts. I had no choice but to accept the warmth of the hospitable Tyroleans—the people of Austria who had invited me. In the back of my mind, my war story swirled: sixty some years ago I was as good as dead in the eyes of the Austrians, then their search to find the pilot of *Priority Gal*, and the phone call this past year that would change my life forever. I was still alive, after all, even though World War II veterans were dying at a rate of almost a thousand a day in the new millenium.

I had lived a long life. I lived comfortably for the most part, only jumped from a plane one time, and that was because I had to. I wasn't a thrill seeker. I found love, had kids, served my country, and a few nightmares aside, I felt fulfilled and ready for the next leg of this journey.

There are secrets a man takes with him to his grave, things that are never talked about, especially when it comes to war. You go on, somehow. Most did, at least, because what choice did we have? There was no diagnosis known as posttraumatic stress disorder six decades ago—no counseling, no bonuses for survival, no big honors, perhaps a drink on the house from time to time. To make matters worse, soldiers didn't talk about their experiences, even to each other, and there were zero bragging rights afterward. Remorse became guilt's big sister. Mostly we tried to forget, but the memories were always looming, and there were bad days and more bad nights, but we persevered. Sixty something years later I finally had put it all to rest. No one asked anymore because no one cared. The world was all caught up in the ongoing war in the Middle East, and rightfully so. I thought about all those poor young soldiers, and I had to ask, what were we doing there?

At ninety-one years old and a recent widower, it was difficult for me to fathom foreign travel, either alone or with a guest. I was, however, not given a choice. The invite had barely left the Austrian government's mouth, and Izzy was all over the idea of a rededication ceremony like salt on a pretzel. I could live without all the attention, the public displays of affection and emotion. The real meaning of my trip abroad was to finally say thank you to Ander and goodbye to my *Gal,* to do my own brand of thanks for her valor all that time ago.

Our flight over the Atlantic was uneventful. In all honesty I was not fond of being a passenger in an airplane. Once trained as a pilot, to feel comfortable letting someone else control your fate was stressful, but there was no way I could show Izzy I was nervous. After Jimmy's untimely death, she, too, was reluctant to fly. Before we left New Jersey, she told me the only person on earth she felt relaxed flying with was me. If anything went wrong, she was convinced I could take over the controls and land the plane. I hadn't been behind the controls of an airplane in fifty years, but if my daughter had faith in me, then I could accomplish anything.

The ravine near Neustift, Austria, where *Priority Gal* crashed. (*Author*)

Part Seven

The Final Mission

THIRTY-FIVE

W HEN THE PLANE TOUCHED DOWN ON FOREIGN
soil, I had a sense of relief. All those months
of planning and we had safely arrived in Munich,
Germany. What would happen next, I had no idea.
Izzy and I would be in the hands of Dr. Mayer and the
Haas family. There was no turning back, and I felt
Elizabeth's strength propelling me forward to this
piece of destiny. I was relieved there was no welcoming committee—just the familiar historian and his
ten-year-old Mercedes sedan.

Germany was a foreboding country, even in times
of peace for a veteran. Half a century later, it still bore
the resemblance of a place that had succumbed to the
dark veil of war. There were still so many bad memories associated with the likes of Munich, Berlin, even
Frankfurt. I know someday down the road, when folks
like me are all departed, Germany will have been

redeemed by the world. For me, it wasn't my favorite place to visit. Returning to the very same valley where *Priority Gal* crashed, and where I bailed out and was taken prisoner, didn't exactly appeal to me, either, but it was the only way I could complete my story. Maybe the nagging feeling would go away when I finished this one last adventure. I convinced myself I was still alive because I wasn't ready to die yet. I had something I needed to accomplish and this had to be it, a return visit to the place most traumatizing. I knew I wasn't crazy. This closure could mean the end of a very long story. Maybe instead of Izzy, I should have brought a therapist, I joked to myself.

The rolling countryside and mountainous land-scape made for a scenic drive from the airport to our Austrian destination. I wished Elizabeth could be here with us, but it wasn't meant to happen that way, I reasoned. Having Izzy along gave the trip an entirely different feel, and I was getting a kick out of seeing her enjoy herself. I was being given an opportunity to show my daughter the places I had been talking about all those years.

Our first stop, just over the Austrian border, was a Hofbräuhaus situated up on the rocks overlooking a large stream running along the base of a mountain range. The colors were exquisite in a view full of lush evergreens and clusters of wildflowers. The tavern was crowded for two o'clock in the afternoon, and we grabbed a seat outside, so Izzy could take some pictures of the breathtaking views.

After finishing off a couple of desserts we all shared from a center plate, a custom I'd have to get used to, I assumed, we left the establishment and returned to high speeds on the autobahn. Next stop was a modest farmhouse, a sign above the front door read: 1762.

Dr. Mayer's ninety-six-year-old mother greeted us at the door and graciously invited us in for a shot of schnapps, as she put it. The woman spoke almost no English, but I could tell by her mannerisms, she was happy to see her son and meet his friends. I had practiced a few select phrases in German, and I was waiting for the right time to try one out. My opportunity came when we said goodbye to Jakob's mother, and I embraced her and said *"Ich liebe dich"* affectionately, *I love you.* I can't imagine the last time a man close to her age said something like that to her, but it had to have been a while. Her cheeks turned red as plums, and she smiled broadly for the first time during the visit, revealing toothless gums. In the Mercedes Dr. Mayer assured me that I had made her year.

The sun was beginning to set when we arrived at the hotel. Mr. and Mrs. Ander Haas, with their eldest son, Peter, greeted us outside. Ander Haas and I embraced, and he looked at me straight on.

"Thank you," he said and grabbed my hand between both of his palms. "Thank you so much for what you did."

"You too, friend, you too." We embraced again.

Ander Haas was of short stature but looked every bit as sturdy. He had a round jolly face with rosy

Ander Haas, right, his wife Christine, Jakob Mayer, and Peter Haas, left. (*Author*)

cheeks and a bristly chin. From head to toe he wore proper Tyrolean garb, including a felt hat donned with a feather. Dr. Mayer insisted on taking a few pictures before we went inside, and Izzy followed suit with her camera. The view of the Austrian-Swiss Alps was spectacular at dusk.

Inside the hotel Peter bartended and served up the liquor of Neustift, proposing a toast to our visit. Then the accordions came out, and a trio of musicians began to play lively Bavarian tunes. Christine, Ander's wife, danced around the room singing. Ander's two granddaughters, dressed in matching smocked dresses—Julia, four, and Therese, seven—performed a classic Tyrolean dance for me as the crowd cheered. I was treated to platters full of fresh relish, cheeses, meats, and warm bread. Everyone seemed genuinely pleased we were there and showed us the utmost hospitality.

I finally retreated to my room after doing a "Supchak Shot," one of the house specials. Izzy stayed behind, engrossed in the attention she was receiving from Peter's younger brother, Gephardt. My assigned room was cozy and clean, with all the amenities of a five-star hotel. I laid down on the soft white duvet, and the jet lag associated with high-speed travel into different time zones was unavoidable, and I was asleep within minutes.

THIRTY-SIX

A S MUCH AS I ANTICIPATED THE DREADED nightmares I might have returning to this place, sleep came easy that first night in Austria. July in Neustift was remarkable, and the lush scenery was breathtaking. When I woke in the morning at 5:30 a.m., I felt refreshed and ready for a day full of Austrian hospitality. I showered, shaved, dressed, and straightened the room before opening the curtains.

The sun was just coming up over the Alps on the Hungarian border, and when I stepped out onto the balcony, I was consumed by the fragrance of fresh flowers overflowing from baskets hanging from the terrace. The view was lit up from behind in hues of purple, pink, and orange. Not by coincidence, my balcony overlooked the exact pasture I landed in sixty some years before. I stood for a while, cane in hand, remembering that day and wondering how in the hell I ended up back here.

Wanting to get a different perspective, I locked up and left my room. I slid a note under Izzy's door that I would be down on the main level of the hotel. If I knew my daughter, I knew I wouldn't see her for at least another two hours. I made my way to the lobby and decided to take a look around.

The lobby was empty except for the bread man, who asked me a question twice, and all I could do was shrug. Perhaps I should have brushed up on my German. At least a smile is universal, and the bread man and I shared one before he placed a large wicker basket on the registration desk and left the inn. I peeked under the linen cloth covering the basket to find all different shapes and types of warm fresh bread. It gave off an aroma I could only have dreamt about in prison camp. I decided I could use some coffee and made my way around back to the spacious dining room.

I discovered a beverage setup—coffee, tea, and an unusual but appetizing assortment of morning condiments, from nutmeg and marshmallows to honey and rock-candy stirrers. I found some bone china cups and matching saucers, and just as I was about to take a seat near the door, Peter Haas came out from the kitchen, clad in a white chef hat and a bibbed apron tied at his narrow waist.

"Ah, Colonel Supchak, good morning! Sleep well?" This was one of the most cheerful men I had ever met.

"Slept like a baby, thanks. The room is very comfortable." I wasn't a fan of hotel stays, but as they went, this one was top of the line in accommodations, so far.

"Come, if you will. Join me in the kitchen while I prepare for the day," Peter graciously said. "I will make you a nice breakfast."

"Oh, no, that's not—"

He didn't let me finish. He picked up my coffee cup from the table, filled it to the brim again, and gestured for me to follow. "Don't be ridiculous! I am going to make you eggs, you like eggs?"

"Sure." I resigned to allow him his indulgences. He seemed to be getting a kick out of having some company this early in the morning. It was obvious he had chosen his career based on what he was exceptional at, hospitality, and he was quite successful.

The hotel kitchen was spotless. As a food handler myself, it's the first thing I look for. Peter pulled up a stool and prattled on about the plans they had for my return. He told me a little bit about the guests who were staying in some of the other rooms. One room had a relative of Arnold Schwarzenegger. Another room had a couple on honeymoon from Connecticut, and he mentioned their name as though I knew the entire East Coast population personally. He explained that the hotel guests were invited the following day to the rededication ceremony. Peter would provide transportation up the mountain for those who didn't hike. Of course, he assured me, Izzy and I would be taken by private car with his dad to the ceremony. I was amazed at his mastery of the English language until I discovered he spoke eight languages. He claimed he had to learn them if he wanted to be an international hotelier.

When he served me my breakfast right there in the kitchen on the stainless steel countertop, I was at a loss for words when he told me he had used three eggs. My thoughts immediately returned to Bassing-bourn and the large breakfast of three eggs that Krusan commented about sixty years before. That breakfast in the mess hall that morning kept me going for a while until young Ander brought me food in the outpost cell. I had never told anyone the story of the three eggs I had for breakfast that day, even after I returned from prison camp. It seemed only significant to me.

When Izzy finally showed up for breakfast, Peter had set the dining room, and one of the tables had a propped plate with "Supchak Familie" written on it. I told her about the three-egg thing, and she thought for a moment.

"You know, Dad, you have a lot of threes associated with the war: three eggs, thirty-three missions, then, of course, there's three kids, and now three eggs today." She sipped her tea after melting two rock candy sticks into it. "I say you play three in the lottery when we get home." True to form, like her mom, my Izzy was an idealist.

The plan for our first full day was for us to take a tour of an aviation parts factory in Innsbruck. It was by private invitation, and Dr. Mayer assured me it was a special invitation I didn't want to miss. I had learned in prison camp that fear of not knowing was the worst kind, so I was a bit nervous about this unsolicited invitation from a complete stranger. I told Izzy while she finished her pancakes about my trepidation.

"C'mon, Daddy, these folks are giving you the hero's welcome, the key to the country sort of honors. What would Mom say, huh?" I listened, wanting to hear Elizabeth's voice more than ever now that I couldn't: *Don't wear white shoes after Labor Day, use your cane both indoors and out, drink OJ every day at three, hold on in the shower.* And yeah, she said I looked like Gregory Peck. I was her hero, and she loved my hands. Sure, Elizabeth would want me to enjoy the trip. She had seen herself as a burden, and perhaps that's one of the reasons she is no longer with us. She was having trouble getting around the house, and now that I was in Austria, I realized with sadness that this trip would have overwhelmed her.

Right on schedule, at 9:30 a.m., Dr. Mayer and his trusty Mercedes arrived as our escort for the day. Ander Haas joined our table for a brief conversation;

he had just completed his hike up the mountain, and he had to get to work. When Dr. Mayer told Ander we had visited Mayer's mother's house the day before, of course Izzy had to share how I made Jakob's mother blush by saying: *"Ich liebe dich."*

While Dr. Mayer began explaining the historical relevance of his mother's house to Izzy, I spoke with Ander, with Peter acting as translator. Unlike his sons, Ander spoke very little English, but he was versed in Chinese, Hungarian, and Russian. While Ander ate his breakfast of pickles rolled in salami and cheese and smiled up at me every so often, what I recognized in his slate-blue eyes were the very same things he saw in my brown eyes: gratitude and warmth. We both knew that we would not be enjoying breakfast in these estates-turned-inns if *Priority Gal* had careened through the streets so many years ago. Would his wife Christine, born and raised in Neustift, have survived the crash? Ander's sisters and his mother? If the town had been destroyed, it would have changed so many things in so many ways. I too may not have survived if Ander and his aunt had not come to my aid.

After breakfast Ander took Izzy and me for a tour of the hotel, and when we got down to the ground floor, where the gym and game rooms were located, Ander proudly showed us to a small gallery dedicated to *Priority Gal.* He had parts of the bomber—rather large parts—mounted on pedestals, with small descriptive narratives below each item.

All I could do was humbly shake my head. I was honored to learn the tavern had a drink named after me, but this . . . this was over the top. It was evident Ander had spent much money and time in excavating, cleaning, identifying, and then creating a showpiece with all of it. There were articles that were written over the years in which Ander discussed the American pilot and the buried bomber. He vowed someday he would thank the pilot in person, and Ander was a man of his word.

Following our tour of Ander's gallery, we reconvened in the parking lot of the inn. Dr. Mayer discussed with Ander our itinerary for the day, and although I didn't understand what they were saying, I knew we were in good hands. Before Ander set out on foot to his place of business at the top of the Alps, he grabbed my hand, and with a big smile pulled me in and hugged me tight.

THIRTY - SEVEN

B ACK ON THE AUTOBAHN, I SAT IN THE PASSENGER
seat while Izzy leaned through the middle from
the back and kept the conversation with Dr. Mayer as
we rolled at a clipped pace. I was grateful for the
reprieve because I was overwhelmed myself. Trying to
process all that was happening, and all the attention
being lavished on me, was not anything I was used to.
I wanted to come across as gracious and humble, but
all the while I desperately tried to keep my swirling
emotions at bay.

On our way to the factory we made a pit stop in
the city of Innsbruck, home of the 1960 and 1976
Winter Olympic games, situated on the border of
Neustift. We rode a glass elevator up to the top of a
needle-shaped skyscraper and enjoyed schnapps,
whose fumes were enough to get one high, and the

best Bavarian pretzels I'd ever tasted. A photographer with two poodles in tow, one black and one white, took several pictures of me on the terrace of the needle overlooking the Austrian countryside.

On one side of the circular terrace, I was able to get a great view of the exact spot where the Olympics had taken place. Even in summer there remained a massive half pipe, for lack of a better word, obviously used for ski jumping. The entire Olympic village was spread out before me, another piece of history.

The streets in the old part of Innsbruck were still cobblestoned in places, and we saw the famous Golden Roof, the centuries-old residence of the Tyrolean sovereigns. Our reststop over, we purchased a few souvenirs and met back at the Mercedes.

As we approached the Italian border, Dr. Mayer pulled his car off the road and stopped in front of electric gates that blocked a long drive. A man in a security-type hat exited a small booth that I hadn't noticed, and when our escort rolled down his window and explained that we were there to see the CEO, the guard waved us in, and the gates seemed to open on their own. I turned just in time to see the fencing come back together behind me, and a chill ran up my spine. The feeling of anything closing me in was a threat to my freedom, and I was a bit unnerved not knowing exactly where we were going or what Austrian citizen we were going to meet.

"How do you know this place?" I asked as calmly as possible. "Why here?"

"To be honest, I've never actually met the man we are going here to see. He contacted Ander when he learned you were visiting Austria and requested that you visit him at his factory." Dr. Mayer didn't sound the least bit concerned. "I've heard of the man, though. He's considered a legend in these parts. He owns this property, along with several Italian restaurants and a radio station situated on the Italian and Austrian borders. Few people have actually met him. He's sort of a recluse. When he goes to dinner, he rents the entire restaurant for him and his guests."

The gravel driveway was lengthy, but the copses of trees eventually gave way to a large building with the outer appearance of a research lab, with most of the structure rendered windowless. Not my favorite type of façade, but I was relieved to see a parking area full of all types of foreign-made vehicles. Not just Mercedes, but BMWs and Volvos and Volkswagens. The place was apparently handsomely populated, and I was a bit relieved until I saw a few armed guards posted along the factory perimeter.

It was very odd, the sense of paranoia I was experiencing being back in that part of the world. Maybe I watched too much news, or the memories were too harrowing to conjure back up, but whatever it was, I felt clammy. Thank goodness Izzy was with me and kept me from backing out, using an excuse that I didn't feel well, or that I was tired. That was one of the good things about getting into my nineties. I could get away with just about any behavior—make lame excuses, and people would understand.

Before I had a chance to take my thoughts any further, we were entering through an "authorized only" door and heading up a large cement set of gray stairs typically found in industry. The place was immaculate. On one side, through a large set of sliding-glass doors, was what appeared to be several small assembly lines. The doors parted, and we were given a brief tour by one of the guards of the airplane parts factory. I was fascinated with the process, having been an engineer for a good portion of my adult life.

"Why the secrecy, the armed guards?" I whispered to Dr. Mayer when the tour was over, and we exited the back through the glass doors. Before Dr. Mayer could respond to my question, a booming voice came up from behind us.

"Welcome, Colonel!" A large man around sixty lumbered toward the three of us, meaty hand extended in my direction. "How the hell are you? Good to finally meet you."

I reached for the man's hand, and he grasped mine in both of his. A smoking cigar hung from his lower lip like he was a cartoon character. He had a broad smile and teeth resembling an exhumed corpse, but I immediately liked the man.

"Wolfgang Deutsch at your service." The man bowed, and a clump of grey ash fell to the shiny buffed floor at our feet. "Come into my office where we can chat." With that, he slung his arm around my shoulders and guided me to another set of steps to a door at the top. Izzy and Dr. Mayer may as well have been invisible. This Deutsch character, in his heavy German accent, wanted my complete attention.

His office was small and modestly furnished. A German shepherd dog greeted him, and at the snap of Deutsch's fingers the dog immediately heeled. The man politely offered us a variety of cold beverages. I declined, and before Dr. Mayer and Izzy could respond, Deutsch continued speaking only to me.

"I want to share something with you. Only about fifteen people have ever seen it, Colonel, and I would be honored for you to be the sixteenth."

"What is it you want me to see?" I leaned forward on my cane, trying to give the impression I wasn't in the mood for games, but my curiosity was piqued. This man knew how to draw out the drama. He was enjoying the dumbstruck looks on our faces.

"I will show it to you in due time. However, there is only one stipulation." He leaned back in his chair, and the leather crackled under his bulk. "You can never tell anyone what you've seen."

"I am only going to involve myself in this if my daughter and Dr. Mayer can share it with me, whatever it is you're talking about."

"Of course your daughter can be by your side the whole time." With that, he pushed a small black book across the desktop. The book was padded and leather bound, and the cover simply read, "Guests," in gold calligraphy. I reached for the book, but before I could put my hand on it, his hand reached under mine, and I halted.

"We have a deal, right? You never met me." His deep blue eyes seemed to drill down into mine to confirm his trust in me. Izzy cut in.

"It's all a little cryptic, but sure, we'll sign the book and pretend we never met you. In fact, Deutsch is probably not even your real name."

He narrowed his eyes on my daughter.

"And that's quite alright, too. Mum's the word." Izzy made a pantomime of zipping her lips shut, and I smiled inside.

After Izzy signed and passed the quill to me, I took my time signing while discretely scanning the names above mine. I tried to show no expression when I read the names of U.S. ambassadors, senators, and several foreign dignitaries whose names I recognized. We were all guests, but to what? I still didn't have a clue. When I attempted to pass the quill and book over to Dr. Mayer, Deutsch stealthily interceded and snatched the book and pen.

"No offense, partner." Deutsch put a hand up as if to signal "halt" and spoke to Dr. Mayer. "The colonel deserves to see what I got behind that door. I invited him and his daughter here, and I appreciate you driving them, but I can't let you sign. You can wait in the lounge with Aggie Boy," and at that the dog trotted to the exit door and sat. Dr. Mayer left the room, and I couldn't help but feel sorry for him, even though he didn't seem to be put off.

When it was just Izzy and me left, Deutsch gestured behind him to what I had assumed was an elevator door when we first came into the office. This eccentric CEO was going to show me something behind those steel doors in utmost confidence, and all I could feel was relief that Izzy was with me. How the hell could I believe that I had this bizarre, surreal encounter with Wolfgang Deutsch unless I had a witness?

THIRTY-EIGHT

WOLFGANG DEUTSCH GUIDED US OVER TO A small box on the wall, containing an intricate security system that scanned his eye. When the elevator doors parted, only to be met with another set of doors. Izzy stayed close behind me, and we followed the man through two more sets of locked doors. The last set of doors opened into what can only be described as a windowless and massive warehouse. It was impossible to take in the entire space at one time.

"Welcome to my resurrected World War II museum," Deutsch proudly announced, sweeping his arm around in a presenting wave. "You are looking at close to a billion dollars' worth of war memorabilia. The Smithsonian would have a coronary if they saw what I am in possession of. If you notice, the air in this specially sealed room is cool and ionized. It keeps all the contents well preserved."

We were standing on a ledge perched about thirty feet up, face-to-face with a perfectly constructed scale model B-17 hanging from thick cords attached to steel ceiling girders. The platform we were on then began to slowly descend, and we were gently let off on the floor. There was very little space not taken up by a showcase of some sort or another. Deutsch had the permanent look of a guy who had just won the war.

Everywhere that I looked were rebuilt planes and military equipment, all in great condition. The showroom was shared equally by German and Allied memorabilia. There were unopened packs of cigarettes, numerous guns, and other weaponry. Canteens, uniforms of all sorts, and missiles were propped on stands and hung from the ceiling. A buzz bomb adorned the very center.

We must have been in that museum for two hours. It was impossible for me to walk the showroom and take in everything. As one would find in a public museum, there were small reenacted stills of wax soldiers in different battles. Each one told a very real and detailed story. The original photos and movie footage, available for perusal, was astounding, and I found that part the most disturbing to view. Deutsch followed Izzy and me around, and for the first time since we met him, he didn't utter a word. He smoked his cigar, continuing to ignore the trail of thick cigar smoke and ash he left in his wake.

He allowed me to give my daughter a private tour of everything I could recall from that time in my life. Izzy didn't say much, but I noticed she had a small journal in her hand and was jotting down notes. She snapped a few photos, but Deutsch limited the things that he allowed her to photograph. He seemed especially partial to preventing the exposure of his Nazi memorabilia.

I was sure we were underground at this point, somewhere in Austria, and I wondered how this man got all this stuff into the warehouse. There was no obvious door to accommodate such massive pieces of military equipment. Mr. Deutsch was correct in his assumptions that the Smithsonian would have a field day in this hideaway. I wanted the opportunity to get some answers from this quirky war buff.

After the tour, we made our way up to a second terrace much wider than the platform we had ridden down on. There was a circular bar area with tables and chairs donned with wax figures emulating an officer's club scene. Izzy and I were shown to seats at the bar, and Deutsch got behind it and began pouring us more schnapps, only his bottle had small flecks of gold floating around at the base.

"Good for the joints!" he proclaimed as he threw back the first shot, as if testing it for acceptability before pouring Izzy and I our own.

"So, if you don't mind me asking, Mr. Deutsch, how the hell did you get all this stuff in here and manage to keep it a secret?"

Henry Supchak with Wolfgang Deutsch in his private underground World War II museum. (*Author*)

He gave a belly laugh, then poured himself another drink, and pulled up a stool opposite us. "My father was a Nazi. I don't know all the details of that sordid ordeal, but he was one of Hitler's cronies. My mother was opposed to the war and forced me to go live with a cousin in Switzerland. I had been fortunate enough to be spared the atrocities of World War II, but when I returned home after four years, I saw the devastation left behind. Austria was in shambles, and I couldn't understand why my father participated in such horrific destruction of his own country." He paused and emptied his shot glass.

Deutsch continued his story. "I was just a boy when the war ended, and my father returned to reclaim his property right on this very spot. He began collecting odd things that he found lying around in abundance at the end of the 1940s. He built this underground storage area and then over time reconstructed several military vehicles. It became a hobby of my father's, but one that his own family didn't even know about. I can only assume that he had to keep the place a secret if he wanted to hang onto it, or, worse, be found with controversial Nazi paraphernalia and be charged with sedition.

"He fronted the warehouse with a legitimate air-craft parts factory, and we only found out what he had been doing all those years after he passed away. As his only son I inherited the business, including the fac-tory. At first, after my discovery of the warehouse, I was horrified and wanted to get rid of the entire lot. It would have taken me years and a large sum of money to dismantle everything and cart it off in the night. So instead I locked it down and kept it tucked away for several years, while the factory in front con-tinued to thrive."

"This is a gold mine." It was all I could think to say.

"Oh, I could never sell any of this stuff. I'm ashamed to admit that my father may have killed Americans to acquire some of this stuff. Collecting World War II memorabilia has become my passion, and in time, maybe before history repeats itself, the museum can be made public. Unfortunately the world is not yet healed from that horrific war. There are still more than seventy-four thousand men who never made it home and whose bodies were never even recovered. How can I in good conscience make a dime off of this place? I have a grandson who just turned two. He doesn't know it yet, but he will inherit this factory and all its dark secrets when he turns thirty and I'm long gone, and he can do with it what he wishes. Meanwhile, it will stay in the family as long as my legal bequeaths are abided by to the letter."

We slowly made our way back across the vast space to the platform, where we would be returned to the waiting Dr. Mayer, whom I hoped hadn't deserted us. Before we stepped on the platform for the ride up and out of the museum vault, Mr. Deustch presented me with a hat with the emblem from his factory, embossed above the brim. I expressed my appreciation for the private tour and thanked him profusely for not just his hospitality, but for sharing his long-kept secret. His last request was for Izzy to take a photo of him and me together in front of the Austrian flag hanging by the exit. There we stood, new acquaintances, arms around each other's shoulders—he with an unlit cigar stub stuck between his lips, and me in my new hat. The shot, he said, would garner a special space on his private museum wall.

THIRTY-NINE

BY TWO O'CLOCK THAT AFTERNOON, WHEN WE were back on the speedway for the hotel, I was suddenly exhausted. It had been a strange day thus far, and I had no choice but to just go with it and enjoy myself. I was relieved that there would be just enough time for me to take a short nap before we had to prepare for dinner in Italy with Mr. Deutsch and his wife, Ursula—in private, of course.

Back in the hotel tavern, I enjoyed filling Dr. Mayer in on my time with Deutsch without really telling him anything at all. Dr. Mayer didn't push for more information, behaving as if had I confided Deutsch's secret to him, Deutsch would have caused trouble for Mayer. This trip was turning into a rare and unique adventure, or at least that was what I believed. Izzy, on the other hand, behaved as though she met men like Deutsch every day, and when I headed up to take a snooze, she was headed out of the front doors of the hotel with Peter's brother, Gephardt, in tow—headed for some shopping.

I slept like a rock, and when I woke to Izzy's knocking on my door, I groaned to signal that I was awake. For a split second I forgot where I was. It slowly came back—the soft white goose-down comforter; the heavy wooden accoutrements; thick, tapered bedposts casting shadows across the ceiling. Austria. I was in Austria. Deutsch had not been a dream. Izzy was waking me to get ready for an Italian-Bavarian dinner in some restaurant where we'd be the only guests in the entire establishment. I wondered if Deutsch would have Mayer wait in the car.

On the way to dinner we took back roads that wound around and were just narrow enough for the Mercedes to pass through. Mayer ripped around bends and corners, and I found that my only consolation was that since our arrival, I had yet to see an accident, not a one. Come to think of it, other than the armed guards at the parts factory, I hadn't seen any sort of law enforcement. I didn't know if that was a good thing or not, but I'll admit, I was well on my way to becoming a religious man by the time we pulled into the lot.

As was expected, the restaurant was empty except for the servers. We were ushered by an adorable blonde hostess, who surprised me when she pulled out my chair. At the head of the table sat Wolfgang

Deutsch, cigar smoke clouding his complexion. He acted thrilled to no end that we were joining him and his wife.

Ursula was a dark beauty in her fifties, thick lips and a smile that made her husband's stained smile even worse in contrast. She was seated next to Izzy and they hit it off instantly—complimenting each other's outfits, shoes, and jewelry. Ursula handed my daughter a box wrapped in lavender paper. Izzy opened it to find inside a delicate crystal butterfly made of Swarovski crystal.

"Butterflies are considered good luck when flying because they are the one species that doesn't crash." Ursula spoke with a beautiful accent.

I could tell Izzy was honored to receive such a sincere gift. She thanked the Deutsches probably more than she needed to. Luckily, she was interrupted when the waiter came for our order, and I realized I hadn't looked at a menu. Of course I wasn't surprised at all when Deutsch, true to form, ordered for all of us.

"Weiner schnitzel, sauerbraten, and kartoffel for all," he told the waiter.

I looked at him astonished. How the hell did he know what *Hauptmann* Metcalf had for lunch while he interrogated me sixty years ago? It was impossible. Deutsch must have seen the look on my face.

"You have to be treated to some authentic Austrian food on your visit, and there's no better place to get it than here. I own the joint." He puffed on his lit cigar, and his face was momentarily gone again. I didn't care much for cigar smoke, especially when eating, but for some reason his smoke didn't bother me. It didn't seem to bother Izzy, either, and she hated smoke.

"Sounds delicious," I said, feeling as though I were left out of a joke. Maybe that meal was the most common food in Austria, like cheeseburgers were to Americans. I didn't know, so I said, "When you come visit us in New Jersey, we'll take you to one of our favorites. How does that sound?"

"Oh," Ursula sighed. "Wolfie doesn't fly. He's afraid of flying. If he has to travel locally for business and is forced to take a flight, he needs to be medicated. There's no way he can travel across the ocean."

"She's right," Deutsch chimed in. "Hate flying, always have."

"But you have an aviation museum?" Izzy sounded incredulous.

"Yes, yes, I do. But we weren't going to talk about that, were we?" Deutsch was teasing Izzy, but she looked petrified about possibly divulging his secret room.

The rest of the meal's conversation was relaxed and interesting, the food was delicious, and when it was time for us to go, Ursula gave Izzy a box of Italian desserts to enjoy back at the hotel. We posed for a few photos in the vacated foyer of the restaurant and then said our final goodbyes.

We drove back to the hotel in silence, Dr. Mayer diligent as ever at the wheel on the hairpin turns and bumpy roads. The tavern was loud and lively upon our return. A trio of accordion players were dancing around from table to table entertaining the patrons with Tyrolean songs.

I remembered my accordion from childhood. It was easy over time to lose touch with memories. It seemed that the good memories we lost, and the bad ones we hung onto. Before turning in for the night, Izzy and I sat for a spell in the tavern and listened to the music resonate around the room while the crowd danced and sang along.

FORTY

WHEN I WENT TO BED THAT NIGHT, THE MOON was in a place that sent beams of light through my open window and illuminated the pasture below. I was in a strange room, in a foreign land, and I never felt more serene.

I woke up that morning and reminded myself it was July 31, and I was still in Austria. It was the morning of the rededication ceremony, scheduled for 11:00 a.m.—the exact time I fell out of the sky and into Austria's backyard. They had a surprise planned for me. I hated surprises as much as the next guy, so Izzy warned me to be gracious. When she said I may want to prepare a short speech, I told her to knock it off; she wasn't helping my anxiety.

I dressed in a tie and the only suit jacket I owned—the burgundy one Elizabeth made me purchase a few years back. I recalled mocking the color, saying I looked like Liberace. I told her it was foolish at my age to buy an expensive, tailored suit unless she was planning on burying me in it. In hindsight I knew my joke didn't sit well with all her fears, so I packed the jacket and was glad I had it in a pinch. It was another tiny piece of Elizabeth that I could carry along with me.

After another delicious breakfast, compliments of Peter, Dr. Mayer arrived and introduced Izzy and me to a reporter for a German television station. His job, the reporter explained, was to record on video our activities of the day. Segments of the rededication would be broadcast during the news program that evening. After lunch Dr. Mayer, Izzy, and I drove to the area where the monument was located. A sizeable group of villagers from Neustift and vicinity, including dignitaries from Innsbruck and Munich, had assembled.

The dedication ceremony and the festivities that followed were held outdoors on a beautiful, warm Tyrolean day, at a classic Austrian roadside inn, just off an unpaved road that also served as a trail, which people could enjoy. All day it had been populated by persons from all over the world who just happened to be hiking the trail, and who stopped to find out what the commotion and the abundance of television cameras were all about.

Looking out from the inn's veranda and across the road is a wide, rocky, ravinelike depression approxi-

Henry Supchak and Ander Haas in 2007, at the place where they first met by chance in 1944. (*Author*)

mately fifty yards below the level of the roadway. I was melancholy. Ander Haas stood at my side, he too staring out at the ravine. He gestured for me to follow him away from the cameras, and together we took a little walk down to the split-rail fence.

In the simplest English we could share, Ander told me the story of his life, and I told him the story of my own. He showed me the burns on his forearm and shin, scars that had faded to ridges over time. When

Ander readied for his day and saw the burns, he thought of me, who I was, and where I was. He claimed my being present for the rededication made the whole thing come full circle.

We stood together on the far side of that wide gravelly path. Beyond the weather-beaten fence, the soothing sound of babbling water echoed among the sounds of wildlife. There was a serene beauty that had not been there—or that I simply hadn't noticed—on my last trip through this powerful region of the world. Billy goats sunbathed and hikers with backpacks and walking sticks made their way day after day, while cool, crystal-clear glacial water ran over the peaceful, majestic grave of *Priority Gal.*

Dr. Mayer interrupted the private moment to inform us that the governor was ready to do the honors. We made our way to the bronze plaque inscribed in German. It is anchored to a huge glacier rock that geologists had determined moved down from nearby mountains—slowly over a few million years—to come to rest at its very location. The ceremony began with brief speeches (mostly in German) and some in broken English. Mayer stayed close to us and interpreted what each speaker was saying. I understood "B-17," "pilot," "Lieutenant Colonel Henry Supchak," "hero," and "thank you." It didn't matter. I knew the Austrian people were genuine in their efforts, and I bowed in thanks when a trio of musicians ended the dedication with the American national anthem.

The commemorative plaque first erected by Ander Haas in 2005 and rededicated in 2007. (*Author*)

One of the attendees, a supreme court judge, had the words from the plaque, which were written in German, translated to English. When I listened to what the plaque said, I was deeply touched, and a little more of that unease I had carried since July 31, 1944, slowly slipped away.

> To Remember
>
> On July 31, 1944, around 1315 hours, a four-engine USAAF B-17G bomber (Flying Fortress) fell approximately eighty meters from here after being hit by flak over the Innsbruck air base. Ander Haas and his aunt were hurt by fragments, and the house he was born in was damaged by flying rubble. The pilots, Henry W. Supchak and John S.

Karlac, in a heroic reaction, prevented the plane from crashing into the village, thus avoiding large misfortune, for which all credit is entitled to them. All nine members of the aircrew of this bomber parachuted. They were imprisoned at SS-Mannschaften, and after preliminary interrogations were sent to a prisoner-of-war camp in northern Germany. The bomber was part of a larger force that attacked Munich and was based at Bassingbourn, England (Eighth Air Force of the USAAF, 91st Bomb Group, 323rd Squadron). Their attempted escape to neutral Switzerland was suddenly interrupted by flak from Innsbruck.

Dr. Mayer explained that they included Karlac's name on the plaque, because in 2005 the only information they could obtain about the pilot were those two names. As much as I assured him that I didn't care about the error, Ander said that the plaque would be rewritten correctly. I didn't begrudge Karlac's name on the engraving. It was just unfortunate that he'd never know that he was finally awarded something, even if it wasn't accurate. He may have been able to build a life around it.

FORTY-ONE

THROUGHOUT THAT DAY, PEOPLE FROM ALL WALKS of life stopped by the festivities to share a drink and chat with me. The trio of musicians continually played tunes that were popular and upbeat. According to Christine, the trio was famous in that part of the world. Several times I was interviewed by different news programs, newspaper reporters, and even the guy with the two poodles was there.

At exactly 4:00 p.m., Christine Haas rang the bell outside the tavern to announce that the guests were to come inside and enjoy a buffet and to toast their returned hero. In the dining room of the tavern and inn, the Haas family chefs had prepared tasteful platters of all sorts of Austrian delicacies. I was relieved that the reporters had all taken the hint that it was dinnertime and took their leave. We sat at two massive wooden dining room tables, and I was at the end of the table, where everyone could see me and I could see everyone else. Conversations in attempted English went back and forth and always included me.

I was dining with two former Messerschmitt pilots, in their eighties and curious about this American bomber pilot returning to Austria after all this time. The men had been friends of Ander's father during the war and had both shot down their share of bombers. It was a strange experience talking to those two in particular, sharing similar harrowing combat experiences, and yet we were on opposite sides of the line during the war. At that table in Austria in 2007, we were just three old men who each walked with the assistance of a cane.

The feast was excellent, the kind of food that sticks to the ribs. I was full and sat back and enjoyed the music being played in the tavern. Christine was dancing around the room with Ander, both dressed in Tyrolean garb. It was tough not to wish that Elizabeth was there to dance with me. No sooner had I thought that than Christine came waltzing over and grabbed my hands, and she danced me around the room.

During the coffee and dessert portion of the meal, Dr. Mayer stood up and asked for everyone's attention. He once again thanked me, and I, of course, responded with many "thank yous" around the crowded room. Then, on behalf of the Haas family, he presented me with a brand new violin made in

Tyrol, and inscribed: "From grateful people to our American hero."

Henry Supchak being interviewed by Austrian television. (*Author*)

I had heeded Izzy's warning about having a speech ready. Joking aside, she was right. At some point I figured I would have to say something formal, and I really should at least put a little thought into what I might say. Here it was, my chance to say thank you, and it wouldn't have mattered if I had worked for weeks on a speech. Choked up, at first I couldn't speak. When I was finally able to find my voice, I thanked Ander and Christine Haas for their wonderful hospitality, and Dr. Mayer for being our escort. The truth was, I had been overwhelmed by the extreme hospitality that these strangers were showing me, and I didn't know how to handle it.

Later that evening, back at the inn after a long nap, Izzy came to my room to remind me about the news program. She said a crowd was already gathering in the bar downstairs in anticipation of viewing the news coverage from earlier that day. I had been interviewed by so many different stations that I was not sure which sound bites they might have captured, or if I would even understand the interpretation.

I was aware of trying not to come across as feeble. I realized I was old—very old. Over the past few years I heard my voice break from time to time, and was occasionally at a loss for pulling up the right word or phrase, and I know the people of Austria had invested much time and money in my visit, so it was important that I didn't embarrass myself.

Down in the bar, Peter Haas took me by the arm and gave me a seat right in the center of the crowd. Several folks from Austria, whom I had not met yet, were there to ask me questions and enjoy the evening festivities. The trio of musicians was present, and I wondered if they had ever stopped playing since that afternoon. The entire Haas clan was there as well. It would be a proud moment for them when the patriarch of their family appeared on television.

As always, Dr. Mayer stood in the background, talking about the events as they unraveled. Often I saw a small notepad in his hands, and I assumed he was gathering material for his history book. Izzy took notes as well. She claimed it was for the purpose of sending thank-you notes to everyone who was a part of the trip. I figured that as long as she hit on all of the highlights as reminders, there would be no way I could forget the details when I eventually sat down again to write.

The presence of more fighter pilots gave me pause, but they too were in the same physical condition that I was in, and they came across as humble and apologetic. We all had a job to do during the war. I knew from prison camp that many German soldiers didn't believe in Hitler's philosophies. They just followed what was expected of them, to defend their country. There was only one former Me-109 pilot I felt uneasy around. He didn't ask any questions and kept his head down during my banter with the other former pilots. At one point the man looked up, and his piercing blue eyes met mine. I would never know what secrets that German harbored, but I knew it would be a while before I would forget his stare.

Cocktails were free flowing, and as the room of Tyroleans began to loosen up, singing and dancing started up again in full force. I even found myself singing along to songs that I recognized. The melodic voice of Christine Haas was prominent throughout. Most surprising of all were the tunes that required yodeling. Done in expressive Bavarian style, it seemed to be almost competitive with the men around the bar. I had to laugh when from across the room Dr. Mayer let out a long yodel.

How often during all of this that I thought of Elizabeth and wished she were there with me to share in it all. She had helped me heal enough to face my past, and I don't believe I'd have been in Austria just then if it weren't for her. Elizabeth wasn't there to share it with me. That final piece to make it perfect would always be missing.

At 6:55 p.m., Peter turned on a huge flat-screen television that was behind some folding doors and announced that the 7:00 p.m. news would be starting in five minutes. A roar of cheers went up around the room, and the music trio took a break. At 7:00 p.m. sharp the Austrian news team began their newscast with world news, and it happened to be a very slow news day, comparatively speaking, so they jumped right into local news. The newswoman spoke in Austrian, but the translation into English appeared at the base of the screen. The feature began with a shot of Izzy and me at the dedication, and a caption over our picture read: "He's Back!"

"The people of Neustift are honoring the presence of a distinguished visitor from the U.S., former lieutenant colonel Henry Supchak, World War II pilot of the Air Force B-17 bomber named *Priority Gal*, which was shot down by antiaircraft guns over Innsbruck on this exact day in 1944 and crashed near the town of Neustift. Before parachuting out of the aircraft, Lieutenant Supchak made sure that the massive bomber would avoid crashing into the village of innocent Austrians. For his heroism, the people of Neustift had erected a monument near the crash site in his honor today." There were several current photos and a few old black-and-white war shots. I was pleased that the news also highlighted Ander Haas and his family businesses.

The news feature ended, and again the bar erupted into applause. The trio broke out into an Austrian rendition of "For He's a Jolly Good Fellow." I looked down at the bar in front of me, and the bar patrons had lined up several drinks—three were Supchak

Shots. I felt that I might hurt their feelings if I didn't drink their offerings, so I solicited Izzy to help me. She was more than happy to oblige. After a succession of palm presses and backslaps, the place returned to the same celebrating I had come to expect from these outgoing folks.

FORTY-TWO

THE MORNING OF OUR LAST DAY STARTED OUT with ominous looking clouds, and I hoped that whatever was planned would be indoors. I, as usual, was down at breakfast by 5:30 a.m., and was enjoying the quiet company of Peter while he readied the dining area for his guests. I sipped my coffee and watched the bruised clouds roll by outside the window. I had to admit that I was glad we weren't flying home through those storm clouds and hoped that the next day would be sunny. As a pilot in control of my own destiny and plane, I didn't mind playing with clouds as long as they were puffy and white. A clear blue sky was boring and a dark sky was forbidding. Lost in thought, I heard whistling coming up from behind me, and I recognized that the man carrying the basket was Peter's bread man. Once again I was enveloped in the warm smell of fresh bread and smiled at the man. Peter emerged from the kitchen, drying his hands on his apron.

"Zeke, how are you this lovely morning?" Peter asked.

The bread man groaned, then responded in Austrian, and the two laughed. Peter introduced me to Zeke, and I assumed, in Austrian, he explained who I was.

Zeke's face lit up, and he placed the wicker basket down on the table and took my hand in his for a hearty shake. He said something twice in Austrian. Peter explained that the bread man had been a young boy in Neustift when the bomber hit the mountains. Zeke had watched from the village, and he and Ander had had numerous conversations over the years about it. Zeke wanted to thank me for making it possible for him to be blessed with kids and grandkids.

Izzy joined me for a late breakfast, and while we waited for Dr. Mayer, we talked about the next morning's plan for departure. Dr. Mayer would return us to the Munich airport by 6:00 a.m. for the return flight to Newark. When he showed up for our last full day in Austria, he was anxious for us to get on the road.

Driving slowly through several small villages, Dr. Mayer pointed out various areas of interest. We were enroute to the Innsbruck airport, where the newspeople wanted to do a special photo shoot before I left for home. Every so often there was a break in the clouds, and I noticed Dr. Mayer glancing up at the dark, brooding weather with concern. A deep valley was a tricky piece of geography, and certainly unpredictable when it came to forecasts.

In less than an hour we reached a gated area at the back of the Innsbruck airfield. The airport was of mediocre size, with three lengthy airstrips. The planes surrounding the hangars were of the small variety. I wondered why we hadn't taken a small charter flight straight into Innsbruck on arrival, but as scenic as it would have been, it would've been equally costly.

The gated entrance to the hangar, where the interview was to take place, was opened by a guard, and he directed us to a low-lying building, where he claimed a reporter was waiting for us. After a short walk across a tarmac, we were greeted by a reporter that I recognized from the dedication ceremony and another younger man that I didn't recognize.

The reporter stated that he would like to do a different sort of interview. He then introduced me to the younger man at his side. "Sir, I'd like you to meet David Grolsch, corporate pilot for Swarovski Crystal."

The younger man extended his hand for a firm handshake, and I noticed the embroidered emblem on his shirt that read: "Swarovski Air."

The reporter continued. "Swarovski of Austria has arranged for an in-flight interview, and they have loaned us their top corporate pilot and a four-seater corporate airplane for the interview."

That said, my heart was in my throat. Not only was there very little blue sky, but I wasn't fond of any sort

Henry Supchak speaking with pilot David Grolsch, right, Jakob Mayer, left, and several reporters at the Innsbruck airport. (*Author*)

of aircraft that was small enough to fit itself into a B-17. I tried to maintain a calm exterior, but when I looked over at Izzy, she was shaking her head.

"You go ahead, Dad, you and Dr. Mayer, and I'll wait here and take pictures."

She was putting me on the spot, so I put it right back at her. "Fine, I'll go, but only if you go, Izzy. It would be a shame for you to miss this beautiful scenery from five thousand feet up." I figured that if Izzy were up there with me, I'd have to be brave and conduct myself appropriately, even though I was scared out of my gourd to get into a small plane.

From behind us came a steady whirring noise, and we all turned to see a sleek white Diamond DA40 with red detailing heading across the tarmac in our direction. When the aircraft stopped just a few yards from us, I realized that this was the Swarovski aircraft. I had never seen such a sophisticated compact plane up close, and I was in awe. It was a beautiful sight, with a healthy humming engine.

"Climb in." The corporate pilot, Dave, gestured to the passenger seat of the revved DA40. With some assistance from Dr. Mayer, I hoisted myself up into the cream-colored leather seat. The control panel of the plane looked like nothing that I had ever seen before. I was grateful that my flying days were over, as I would have to learn all the new digital type of instruments, as opposed to the old-fashioned manual panel that I was familiar with.

Dave took his seat in the pilot's chair, and Izzy and the reporter occupied the two seats in the back. Izzy was directly behind me, and when we put the headsets on, I asked how she was doing.

"Wow, I can hear you through these things." I could tell she was a little nervous about this, but I reassured her that it would be a great experience. I hoped that I was correct.

As the plane taxied and then lifted off the ground, I watched Dr. Mayer wave to us from the tarmac and wished there had been more room in the plane for him, but once again he opted to hang in the background for his guests' enjoyment. We were about fifteen feet off the ground, and Dave flipped a few of the tabs and turned to me and released his grip on the gears.

"She's all yours, Colonel."

FORTY-THREE

"DON'T LIKE FLYING WHEN THE CLOUDS HAVE rocks in them," I responded. Instinctually, I reached for my set of controls. I was able to discern a few of the gauges on the panel, and the altimeter read six hundred feet. I was flying a plane for the first time in sixty years, in the most mountainous landscape in the world. I was flying.

"Ha!" Dave laughed. "I like that line, Colonel, clouds with rocks . . . . I think I'm gonna steal it from you." He sounded American, but said that he had been born in Switzerland.

Izzy realized that I was flying the plane when Dave turned around in the pilot seat and offered to take her picture while flying with Dad. "How does it feel to have your old man flying a plane at ninety-two years old?" Dave asked. "Technically, you're not supposed

Henry Supchak at the controls of a private plane in the same sky where he piloted a B-17 bomber in 1944. (*Author*)

to fly after the age of seventy-five in these parts of the world, but we're making an exception for the colonel here because we know he can do it."

"No offense, Dave, but I feel safer with my Dad flying, because I know there is no way he'd ever let anything happen to me."

"I hear you." Dave accepted Izzy's camera, and I saw him take a few profile shots of me and then of Izzy.

I only answered the questions that the reporter asked and didn't contribute to any conversations otherwise because I was high on life at that moment. I was flying a plane, a high-tech aircraft, and I was in command. Dave was a great instructor. "Take it up to five thousand . . . now eight thousand . . . bank it around." The plane was a spitfire. I guided her through the deep-grey shaded crevice of the Austrian Alps like a high-end sports car.

Dave prattled on, pointing out the sights to Izzy. True to form, my daughter kept the conversation going, and there was a tiny place in my brain that wasn't consumed with the fact that I was flying, which heard references to Innsbruck, *The Sound of Music*, Olympics, Mozart, crystal, champagne, chocolate. I had to smile when Izzy said, "What else is there?"

Before we headed back to the airport, Dave pointed out the three inns and the pasture that I had landed in so long ago. I looked down and saw the difference a half a century had made. The scene was no longer war torn and sepia colored; now it looked inviting and colorful.

I brought the plane around and headed in a southern direction back to the airport as per Dave's instructions. It amazed me how little attention he was paying to what I was doing. He spent most of the forty-five-minute joyride with his head facing the backseat. I wasn't complaining. This was indeed the highlight of my entire trip.

It was then, when I readied the plane for landing and Dave told me with complete confidence to take it in, that something washed over me. I was acutely aware of the sixty years of unease that I had carried around with me had suddenly gone. I was somehow lighter, clearheaded, and I heard Elizabeth's voice: ". . . *now go finish your book.*"

As Dave instructed, I took her in. I landed with a few skips and then a smooth touchdown. There was a cheering crowd gathered in anticipation of my return, including Ander and his family. This time they didn't shoot us down—*Priority Gal*, Supchak, Karlac, Krusan, Leahy, Feinman, Thomas, Taylor, Hettler, Sheppard, Skorpik, and Rocco. My plane and crew landed safely this time, and Austria welcomed us with open arms.

EPILOGUE

It has been five years since I returned from my Austrian journey, and I finally finished getting my story down on paper. I did have a sense of true closure when I wrote my last word. I understood that as long as I lived I would never be able to erase my war memories. I also realized that it was those same events that shaped the man I had become. The amazing fact is that I am still learning from those experiences, even as I write.

I shared with Izzy the thousand or so handwritten pages of my memoirs. She offered to type it into the computer for me, so we would have a copy that her boys could read. I trusted her with my work, and a few months later, she presented me with a binder containing nearly one hundred typed pages that became the basis for this book.

Dr. Mayer has visited us in the United States a few times since our return. On his last visit he informed us that Wolfgang Deutsch had passed away. I thought about my signature in his guest book and wondered

what fate would become of that. I also learned from
Dr. Mayer that the Haas family decided to sell a portion of their hotel establishment when the world
economy went south, but the new owners were not
faring well, and sold the property back to the Haas
family for half of what the new owners had paid for it
to begin with. Everything changes unpredictably all
over the world, and not just for me.

The attention for my service to this country has
never ebbed. I am still invited to countless parades,
ceremonies, and school functions. People ask to
shake my hand at least three times a week, just
because I am wearing my Purple Heart cap. Last year
I was invited to a B-17 show held at a local airport.
The young pilots who flew the B-17 to the airport
that day said they had never met a real live B-17
pilot, and if the weather hadn't taken a turn for the
worse, I would have probably been coerced by Izzy to
take the flight that the pilots had offered me. I'd have
had to joke that I hadn't brought my chute with me,
but the truth was that I had no desire to get back into
the B-17. The story of my military life had come full
circle, and I had no regrets. Truth be told, I finally
moved on.

To fill my days, I still write. I write letters, but
mostly I write about my theories on creation and the
universe. Another hobby that I've picked up over the
past ten years is drawing. Creating visual art is one of
my favorite ways to spend time. When you think

you're too old to do anything else, pick up a set of colored paints and go at it, not for anyone else but yourself.

Elizabeth always took great care in remembering everyone's birthdays and sent cards without fail. After she was gone, I carried on her tradition and began making homemade cards for our kids and grandkids. I get a kick out of personalizing them, and if I tape a few bucks on the back of the picture, they're all the more appreciated.

I've also been attempting to learn the violin. It's a tough instrument, but if played properly, I love the sounds it creates. Music has always been a very important part of my life. I can be brought back to a vivid moment forty years ago with Elizabeth just from hearing a particular melody. Funny thing, whenever I hear the song "Edelweiss," I don't think of *The Sound of Music*, I think of Ander Haas. He will always be one of my heroes.

I had wanted to end my story there, and just yesterday Izzy stopped by the house to tell me that she had sent our prospectus out to publishers. Someone wants to publish it. Just when I thought my story at the ripe old age of ninety-six was coming to an end, another incredible journey begins. . . .

INDEX

ACKNOWLEDGMENTS

An enormous amount of credit must go to Dr. Jakob Mayer, a brilliant historian turned friend. Ander Haas and his family are difficult to thank because mere words cannot express how life changing this whole experience has been for our family. The Austrian people were so warm and welcoming, and the hospitality of the Haas family went above and beyond. Ander, you have given Lt. Col. Henry Supchak a legacy that has now come full circle, and for that we will be forever grateful.

I would like to thank Westholme Publishing, including copyeditor Laura Pfost, for her patience and expertise in World War II history; Trudi Gershenov for her beautiful cover design; and our publisher, Bruce H. Franklin, for his attention, sincere enthusiasm, and passion for this story.

I am so fortunate to be a part of the County College of Morris community, where personal and professional growth is always encouraged, and where the bar of excellence is constantly raised. I want to express special thanks to Diane Davis, an amazing woman who has been like a sister to me.

Thanks to the entire Kennedy clan—namely, Jim Allyn for his original song, *Priority Gal*, and to Candace Roberts Ruddy, my very best friend, for her constant encouragement.

Jay, Ryan, and Matt: thanks to the three of you for being the most phenomenal sons a mom could have, and for your understanding and support throughout this process. To Chase, the first person to ever read one of my manuscripts from beginning to end, I miss you and love you like my own.

Last but not least, I thank my mom, Gene Elizabeth Supchak, for always making me first read the book before allowing me to see the movie; for letting me stay up as late as I wanted, even on school nights, as long as I was reading; and for teaching me what unconditional love means.

I don't need to formally thank my dad, Lt. Col. Henry Supchak, because we are so blessed to be able to show appreciation for each other every day. I know he loves me and believes in me. I will always recall with fondness and humility the day dad and I returned from our trip to Austria and I offhandedly commented that this whole experience would make a great book, and he turned to me and said, "Well then, write it."